ARRAN WATER

An Island Whisky History

ARRAN WATER

An Island Whisky History

Gregor Adamson

Foreword by Charles MacLean

First published in 2019 in conjunction with
Isle of Arran Distillers by The Angels' Share

an imprint of Neil Wilson Publishing Ltd
www.nwp.co.uk
www.arranwhisky.com

Paperback edition ISBN 978-1-906000-97-4
Hardback edition ISBN 978-1-906000-98-1
Ebook edition ISBN 978-1-906000-91-2

Printed and bound in Scotland by Bell & Bain, Glasgow.

CONTENTS

FOREWORD

ARRAN IS – OR CERTAINLY WAS – commonly described as 'Scotland in miniature' on account of its topography, which combines both Highland and Lowland scenery. This splendid book reveals that the island was also a microcosm of what was happening elsewhere in the Highlands in relation to illicit distilling and smuggling during the late 18th and early 19th centuries – a fact which has hitherto been overlooked by historians.

Gregor Adamson has done a magnificent job. His research is thorough, even exhaustive, his approach scholarly, his writing lucid and engaging. I learned a lot about a subject which I myself have researched and written about extensively* – indeed, this is the best account of smuggling I have encountered.

It is surprising that the subject has been ignored, for the illicit whisky from Arran was considered by connoisseurs to be second only to the same cratur from the Glenlivet district of what is now called Speyside. 'Private' distilling was only banned in 1781; prior to this individuals or communities were entitled to produce whisky for their own consumption, so long as it was made from grains grown locally and was not offered for sale. Of course, these conditions were often ignored and there was an extensive trade in smuggled whisky (the term embraced both illicit distilling and the transportation of illicit goods), and when smugglers were caught and brought to trial, magistrates were usually lenient. After all, judges were often landowners and if their tenants made and sold whisky they were better able to pay their rents.

By the turn of the 18th century smuggling was endemic. The hard-pressed Excise was incapable of subduing it and the increasingly onerous excise duties, imposed by government to pay for the war with France, simply encouraged distillers to operate outside the law. As Mr Adamson writes: 'By the early 1800s whisky became the chief commodity transported by Arran smugglers as illicit distillation grew to unprecedented levels.' But by then landowners were becoming increasingly concerned that if this aspect of the law could be flouted with impunity then further civil disobedience would ensue. Their fear of anarchy was realised during the turbulent years which followed the conclusion of the Napoleonic Wars and they pressed the government to address the problem by encouraging illicit distillers to go legal. Ultimately this resulted in the Excise Act of 1823 which laid the foundations of the modern Scotch whisky industry.

As I have said, all this was reflected in microcosm on Arran – except the last, the encouragement to open a legal distillery. This did not come about to any meaningful degree until the opening of the Arran Distillery at Lochranza in 1995, which will be followed in early 2019 by the opening of Lagg Distillery in the south of the island by the same company, not far from the original site of a licensed distillery of the same name which operated briefly in the 1820s and 30s.

I commend this book to you wholeheartedly. It is a fascinating and accurate case study of what has become 'Scotland's greatest international ambassador' – and the world's greatest drink!

Charles MacLean, Master of the Quaich
Singapore, January 2019

Scotch Whisky: A Liquid History (Cassell, 2003); *Scotland's Secret History: The Illicit Distilling and Smuggling of Scotch Whisky* (with Daniel MacCannell, Birlinn, 2017)

INTRODUCTION

I T HAS BEEN SUGGESTED that the great Scots poet, Robert Burns, was blind to the natural beauty of his surroundings as he failed to mention the Isle of Arran in any of his literary works, although for many years he viewed the island's scenic grandeur on a daily basis from his native Ayrshire. It could be argued that this ability to turn a blind eye extended to his duties as an Excise officer. Burns' enjoyment of whisky and his disdain for the Excise establishment are detailed throughout his works, most notably in *The Deil's Awa Wi' The Exciseman* and *Scotch Drink*.

The capacity to ignore illicit whisky and Arran was not confined to the exciseman Robert Burns. From the scale of illegal production and consumption on the island it would appear that some of his Excise colleagues were afflicted with the same selective blindness in the late 18th century. Arran was a hub of unlicensed whisky distillation during this period, with almost every island tenant engaged in some aspect of this illicit trade. Distilling was vital to the Arran community, becoming ingrained in the island's cultural and economic make-up.

Islanders considered small-scale distilling a birthright, a craft that had been passed down and perfected for generations. Illicit Arran whisky, commonly known as 'Arran water', was revered for its quality throughout Scotland. Its main market was the Ayrshire coastal towns where it commanded a price equal to, and often exceeding, whisky from the

1

renowned producing districts of Kintyre and Islay. Islanders used a substantial smuggling network to successfully transport the produce of their 'sma' stills' to this mainland market. Smugglers often carried out the dangerous sea crossing at the dead of night in the worst possible weather to avoid the attentions of the hated excisemen and feared Revenue Cutters that patrolled the Firth of Clyde.

Excisemen and customs officers were widely unpopular amongst the majority of the island's inhabitants. There are numerous accounts of violent clashes between Arran smugglers and these so-called 'gaugers', with casualties on both sides. Gaugers were not only obstructed in the exercise of their duty by the ingenuity and cunning of island distillers and smugglers; excisemen on the front line, like Robert Burns, were hindered by ineffective government excise policy which inadvertently encouraged illicit distilling to the detriment of the Revenue and licensed distillers.

By the early 19th century illicit distilling and smuggling had become endemic. There was growing concern amongst the Arran elite that this industry was damaging both the island's commercial viability and the morals of its people. Improvement measures were eventually introduced that slowly eroded the social and economic foundations of the illicit trade. These landowner actions were supported by successful legislative reforms, ending 120 years of excise ineptitude with dramatic implications for Arran distilling and the traditional island way of life.

In addition to its reputation for smuggling, Arran was also home to numerous licensed distilling ventures. In the 1790s, three legal distilleries operated on the island for a brief period. During the boom in small-scale Highland production in the 1820s and 30s, a legal still was also established at Lagg, less than a mile from the site of the new distillery which is currently under construction.

Ultimately, legal whisky production, like so many of the small island industries, ended in failure. By the 1850s, both illicit and legal distilling had faded into insignificance on Arran. Nonetheless, the spirit of the smuggler lived on amongst a few hardy islanders who continued to defy the government into the 20th century. Stills were fired for home consumption often when whisky was scarce and its need was great.

Two centuries ago whisky production was a key element of Arran's economy, in addition to its cultural and social traditions. Distilling remains central to modern-day island life through the success of Isle of Arran Distillers. In the intervening period, however, Arran's rich distilling past was neglected, overlooked by local historians and whisky writers alike. Subsequently, the island's unique distilling story was cast into the shadows of neighbouring whisky-producing areas such as Campbeltown and Islay.

An examination of historical distilling practices on Arran is long overdue and in bringing this project to the wider public, I would like to thank Isle of Arran Distillers who supported it. Thanks are also due to Neil Adams and Ann Gibson of the National Register of Archives for Scotland; Revd Angus Adamson; Robbie Adamson; Susan Adamson; the staff at the Arran Heritage Museum; Mark Bunyan; Rob Burns; Liz Dale; the staff at the Dick Institute, Kilmarnock; Stuart Gough; John Hartley; Kate Hartley; Alan Little; Rab Logan; Charles MacLean; the staff at the Mitchell Library, Glasgow; Euan Mitchell; the staff at the National Records of Scotland, Edinburgh; Richard Oram; Thomas Rees of Rathmell Archaeology; Grace Small and Sophie Taylor. Finally, a special thank you to Mr Charles Fforde for granting me access to the invaluable records held in the Arran Estate Office.

In this book I endeavour to fill the void, and explore, 'the sad, mad but exciting and profitable days,'[1] of smuggling and illicit distilling, arguably one of the most dramatic aspects of Arran's fascinating history.

Gregor Adamson

1

THE ARRAN LANDSCAPE

T HE ISLE OF ARRAN is one of the most distinctive features of the Firth of Clyde. Enclosed in this body of water by Argyll and the Kintyre peninsula to the north and west, and by the county of Ayrshire to the east, Arran is the seventh-largest, and southernmost inhabited island in Scotland. Arran is defined by the Highland Boundary Fault which bisects the island, resulting in fertile farmland and moorland to the south and rugged mountainous terrain in the north. This distinct natural beauty and proximity to the central belt has allowed the island to develop into a popular tourist destination; it seems Robert Burns was one of the few who could resist Arran's unique charms. Nowadays, the island is readily accessible by a short ferry crossing from either Ardrossan on the Ayrshire coast, or Claonaig on the Kintyre peninsula. The island, however, has not always been so easily reached. In the 18th and 19th centuries, Arran was isolated from mainland Scotland due to poor transport links and inadequate landing facilities. As late as 1855 it was lamented that, 'there is not a single wharf on the whole island, and people, cattle, and produce have to be embarked and landed by means of small boats, just as was the custom in the days of Robert the Bruce.'[1]

From 1503 onwards much of Arran was controlled by the Hamiltons, a powerful noble Lowland family. For centuries, they had sought to conserve the island as a private hunting estate for their own enjoyment and the entertainment of the social elite. In 1836, it was documented that, 'The Duke, being desirous of preserving the game in Arran, does not much encourage the residence of strangers.'[2] Early visitors fortunate enough to gain access would have encountered an alien land and way of life, dramatically different to the neighbouring Lowland counties. Although located in southern Scotland, under the ownership of an influential Lowland family, Arran is traditionally part of the Gaidhealtachd.[3] The Arran historian William MacKenzie perhaps most completely sums up the unique character of the island, suggesting that, 'Arran, in fact, does not form part of the Lowland system; it is an outlier of the Highlands in character and relationships. Essentially it is a border land, and only the more artificial political scheme brings it within the Lowland control.'[4]

During the 18th century, Arran's culture and economy was akin to the Hebrides and other isolated Highland regions of Scotland. Subsistence farming and fishing were key elements of the island economy. In the 1700s, communal agriculture was widely practised with the Arran population loosely organised into small settlement units, known as clachans or townships. Each clachan provided subsistence for a number of families who shared ownership of livestock and strips of land for cultivation. In terms of social structure these farming units were organised in a very simple manner. The residents of each clachan worked as a community, organised by an individual who held the 'tack' or lease, referred to as the tacksman. He would collect an annual rent from each family, allowing him to subsequently pay rent for the clachan landholding to the Hamilton estate.

The land held by each clachan was divided and worked as three basic units. Firstly the infield, comprised of the land closest to the clachan buildings. This area was the most fertile as it was regularly manured and annually cultivated. Surrounding this was the outfield, which was cropped by a basic rota. It was ploughed until the crop yield dropped to a point where it was no longer considered worth re-planting. It was then left to fallow or used as grazing for a period, before being returned to the plough. Beyond this was the communal pasture, often hill pasture, on which the farm stock was grazed. The arable land was ploughed using a system known as 'run-rig', derived from the Gaelic 'roinn', translating to, 'a share'. The cultivation of this land was highly labour intensive, using primitive wooden ploughing equipment. The allocation of land in each clachan was carried out by lot, usually on an annual basis, ensuring that no single family could keep the best land for themselves.

The modern villages of Brodick, Lamlash, Whiting Bay, Kildonan, Kilmory, Blackwaterfoot, Pirnmill, Lochranza, and Corrie, did not exist in 18th-century Arran. The majority of the island population lived in the communal clachans clustered around the coastline. This allowed them to supplement their diet through fishing. The largest of these settlements were situated along the southern coast at East Bennan, West Bennan, Shannochie, Torrylinn, Clachaig, Bennecarrigan, and Sliddery. In the 1770s, it was noted that the Sliddery clachan supported over 300 people. There were also significant dwelling sites in the Shiskine glen and at North Sannox, Glen Rosa and Clauchlands. In 1766 there were approximately 100 of these recorded settlements scattered throughout Arran. These clachans were compact collections of blackhouses and outbuildings, which were built out of dry stone, turf and clay with thatched roofs secured with heather ropes. Although unrefined in terms of construction pre-Clearances island dwellings were, 'a fabric of considerable solidity, quite impervious to the weather.'[5] The building of blackhouses was a communal activity, with groups of 12 to 15 island men capable of building one in a day, provided they were refreshed with 'a gallon of whisky.'

A number of clachans can still be viewed at Shannochie (Ordnance Survey map reference NR 979213), Shedog (NR 912301), Mayish (NS 016358), and High Corrie (NS 022423).

They can be identified by the rather haphazard way the houses are laid out. However, the buildings themselves are much more modern than the settlements. Their architecture indicates that they were constructed within the last 150 years. Horace Fairhurst, an expert on the history and archaeology of Arran, noted that there was not a single house on Arran, other than Brodick Castle, that predated the improvement movement of the early 1800s.[6] Therefore, all that remains of the traditional Arran blackhouses are the ruins of abandoned settlements, such as Gargadale (NR 957261) and North Sannox (NS 001468).

Arran residents in the 18th century shared similar cultural traditions with their Highland compatriots. These customs were based on language, communal agriculture, and an intimate knowledge of their natural surroundings. This way of life was becoming increasingly separate from the burgeoning urbanisation and industrialisation of the central Lowlands in the late 18th and early 19th centuries. Although viewed as backward by many agricultural reformers, the extensive working of the land, predominately by hand, allowed generations of Arran residents to forge a unique knowledge and bond with the landscape around them. The Duke of Hamilton's island factor, John Paterson, documented the islanders' affinity with their natural surroundings:

> ... the inhabitants of all wild and elevated regions seem to have a peculiar attachment to their native land. The dread of being expelled from Arran, has more efficiency in restraining those of its inhabitants who may be inclined to dishonest, vicious or idle courses, than all the penal laws in force; and when a stranger marries a woman of the island, the couple are never at rest till they acquire a settlement in the native place of the wife.[7]

Islanders were dependant on the immediate natural world around them and understood its vital importance to their existence. Communal agriculture was critical and the inhabitants of Arran were noted as being, 'remarkably attached to their native soil.'[8]

This idea of a connection between people and place could be construed as a somewhat idealistic notion and there is a danger that comparisons are made with the Romanticism contained in the novels of Sir Walter Scott. Nevertheless, it is important to gain a sense of this connection, in order to fully appreciate and understand the actions of the island's past residents. Their understanding of the landscape allowed them to scrape a living in this often unforgiving and unpredictable island environment. To survive they had to be adaptable and take advantage of all the natural resources available to them. These natural assets became considerably more valuable in the late 1700s. In Westminster, a world so detached from their subsistence way of life, legislative changes were being implemented by the British Parliament that would have a dramatic impact on the islanders preferred pastime – whisky distilling.

2

UISGE BEATHA AND EARLY EXCISE LEGISLATION

THE FIRST WRITTEN REFERENCE regarding whisky in Scotland appears in the Exchequer Rolls from 1494: 'To Brother John Cor, by order of the King, to make aqua vitae 8 bolls of malt.'[1] *Aqua vitae* is a Latin term meaning 'water of life'. In Gaelic, this directly translates to '*uisge beatha*', from which the modern term whisky is derived. John Cor was a monk based at Lindores Abbey in Fife. It has been argued that Irish monks were the first in the British Isles to carry out the practice of distilling and they passed that knowledge across the North Channel to their Scottish counterparts. There is no documented evidence to support this supposition and it has long been a matter of heated debate amongst whisky scholars and enthusiasts.

It can however be declared with great certainty, that aqua vitae was predominately distilled for medicinal purposes during this period. In 1505, a monopoly of manufacture was granted to the Guild of Surgeon Barbers in Edinburgh. This early medicinal whisky would have been quite unlike anything produced by modern-day distilleries. Aqua vitae was more like a course tonic, including various herbs such as mint, rosemary and sage added to improve flavour. Up until the late 17th century on Arran, whisky was certainly consumed for relief from minor medical afflictions. In 1695 the pioneering travel writer Martin Martin conducted a tour of the island, documenting that, 'the natives think a dram of strong waters is a good corrective.'[2] Early Arran whisky was not exclusively produced and consumed for medicinal purposes. The spirit was becoming more widely accepted as a social drink as well as a tonic. As early as the 16th century, islanders were trading their whisky in the neighbouring Lowland counties. In 1590, 15 gallons of Arran whisky was sent from Ayr to Ireland.[3] Undoubtedly, Arran 'uisge beatha' was becoming increasingly important to the island economy for trade purposes.

Throughout the 16th and 17th centuries whisky-making was carried out on a small scale across the island. Over the centuries the practice gradually embedded itself into the cultural fabric of Arran. As was the case in many other Highland regions, distilling came to be accepted as an islanders' birthright, a traditional craft that had been passed down and perfected through the generations. The produce of their stills provided relief for the sick, refreshment during social celebrations and was becoming increasingly valuable as a tradeable commodity. 'Uisge beatha' certainly was the water of life.

As the popularity and availability of whisky increased throughout Scotland, the government sought to control and benefit financially from its production. In 1644, the first tax on spirits was imposed by the Scots Parliament. Duty was levied on, 'everie pynt of aquavytie or strong watteris sold within the country.'[4] This excise action followed the precedent set by the English Parliament in the preceding year when duty was introduced to help fund the royalist army of Charles I during the Civil War (1641-52). The rate of spirit duty has been a matter of controversy ever since this initial levy and has been altered frequently due to changing governments and parliamentary policies. Between 1644 and 1707, the tax on spirits was regularly and substantially increased in an attempt to reduce a perceived rise in excessive drunkenness.

Furthermore, distilling was prohibited in times of poor harvest throughout the 17th and 18th centuries, in recognition that a great quantity of grain was being consumed throughout the country for whisky manufacture. The government outlawed all forms of distilling between March 1757 and December 1760. This had a significant impact on the Arran economy, with 16 tenants in the south-end of the island petitioning the estate factor, James Stewart, for rent abatements. The residents blamed their economic misfortune on, 'the Distillers in this island our ordinary Support for money has our malt in Custody and they being this day [*sic*] Charged and publicly prohibited from Distilling Spirits ... '.[5]

The 1707 Act of Union resulted in further excise reforms. The Scottish Excise was restructured in the mould of the English system. This aimed at equalising the duty on spirits throughout the new United Kingdom of England, Scotland, Wales, and Ireland. The reforms in Scotland saw the English methods initially introduced in Edinburgh and a selection of larger ports and market towns. By 1712, these reforms had been rolled out across Scotland with Excise Collections set up in Aberdeen, Ayr, Berwick, Dumfries, Dundee, Fife, Glasgow, Inverness, Linlithgow, Elgin, Perth, Scrabster, Selkirk, Ullapool, and Wigton.[6]

In 1713, the malt tax was extended from England to Scotland. This was met with violent opposition and when the tax was increased in 1725 there was rioting in Glasgow, resulting in 11 deaths. The introduction of the malt tax reduced the consumption of ale throughout Scotland, as many were put off by its subsequent rise in price and fall in quality. As a result, the popularity of whisky increased markedly, replacing ale as Scotland's drink of choice by the 1760s.[7] Naturally, this stimulated distilling in order to meet the growing demand for malt spirits. The newfound taste for whisky created an incentive to illicitly sell the produce of private small stills. The Excise responded to this quickly, passing legislation that reduced the size of still allowed for private use from ten gallons to two gallons in 1779. Two years later private distillation was outlawed completely. This drove small-scale production in Highland areas, including Arran, underground. Excise officials were given sweeping new powers allowing them to seize spirits and destroy wash and utensils. They could also request military support to suppress what was now regarded as 'illicit' rather than private distilling.[8]

The outlawing of private stills was followed by one of the most notoriously ill-advised pieces of 18th-century government legislation – the 1784 Wash Act. This legislation was introduced by the Westminster government with encouragement from the excise authorities. The act set out to simplify the administration of legal distillery taxation, as well as lowering duty rates in both England and the Lowland areas of Scotland. Furthermore, licensed distillers in the Highlands were regulated under an entirely different system and were charged a lower duty than their Lowland counterparts.

A precise geographical 'Highland Line' was established to separate the two regions of Scotland. Under the act, the Highlands were defined as, 'the several counties of Orkney, Caithness, Sutherland, Ross, Inverness, Argyll, Bute, Stirling, Lanark, Perth, Dumbarton, Aberdeen, Forfar, Kincardine, Banff, Nairn, and Moray.'[9] Arran was included in this Highland zone as a part of the county of Bute. Understandably, Lowland distillers were outraged at the perceived unfairness of this, and the following year the act was amended stipulating that stills in the Highlands could not exceed a capacity of 40 gallons, only grain grown in the parish could be used in malting, the malt used each year was limited to 250 bolls (approximately 15 tonnes), and there could only be two licensed stills per Highland parish.[10] Additionally, to ensure legal distillers in the Highlands did not gain an unfair advantage they were prohibited from exporting their whisky into the Lowlands. The establishment of this Highland-Lowland divide was successful in encouraging legal distilling throughout Scotland.

However, the division provided further stimulus for illicit distilling and smuggling in the Highlands. Unlicensed producers in this region could earn considerable profits by unlawfully transporting their whisky for sale into the expanding Lowland markets. This smuggling trade was further encouraged by many of the larger Lowland distilleries adopting newly developed rapid distillation methods. This involved working shallow stills which produced distillate in minutes rather than hours. This dramatically reduced the quality of Lowland whisky, creating a huge demand for high quality, traditionally distilled Highland 'sma' still' malt whisky in the south of Scotland. This demand could only be satisfied by increased illicit distilling and smuggling due to the exclusion of legal Highland distillers from markets in the Lowlands.

Initially the changing legislation had negative implications for small-scale Arran distilling. By the late 18th century home distilling was common with local historian MacKenzie MacBride asserting that there were 32 private stills on the island in 1784, with 23 of these located at the south-end.[11] Following the passing of the Wash Act, 26 of these stills were, 'collected and carried to the Castle.'[12] The outlawing of home distilling, which had developed into an integral part of the islanders' culture, must have shocked and angered them. In the face of the criminalisation of this key craft industry, Arran residents adapted quickly and used their natural surroundings and the flaws in the new excise laws to their economic advantage.

Distilling activities increasingly took place away from settlements in order to minimise the threat of detection and the confiscation of valuable distilling equipment. The numerous woodland glens of the south-end provided ideal locations for illicit whisky-distilling bothies. The fast-flowing burns that had carved out these natural features over thousands of years provided a pure source of water that was critical to the distilling process. Improving agricultural methods gradually increased yields throughout Arran. In 1772, 148 bolls (9.25 tonnes) of (bear) barley, and 515 bolls (34.5 tonnes) of grain were sown on the island.[13] Much of this was grown in the fertile lands of the southern and western coasts.

The southern district was isolated due to the absence of adequate transport links. The first road on Arran was not constructed until 1810. This so-called parliamentary road only stretched a few miles between Brodick and Lamlash. Seven years later the west coast got its first road connection, as 'the String' was built linking Blackwaterfoot with Brodick. Pier amenities were not constructed until the late 19th century. Consequently, the export of raw materials from the island was difficult. The south-end was serviced by a series of shallow natural harbours, only capable of accommodating small boats. Poor internal and external communications in the late 1700s made the transport of bulky produce, like barley, to nearby mainland markets a challenging undertaking. It was much more prudent to convert grain into whisky which could be shipped to neighbouring markets with relative ease, providing it escaped the attention of the gaugers.

As outlined previously, there was a growing demand for high quality Highland spirits in rapidly expanding Lowland centres, including the flourishing coastal towns of Ayrshire. As a result, Arran whisky could be sold at a price far exceeding the legal Lowland alternative which was becoming increasingly unpalatable. Drinkers of this legal spirit complained that its consumption, 'did not agree with their stomachs; it gave them a great head ache if they took the quantity that they could take of Highland spirits without effect.'[14]

Unsurprisingly, the demand for the distillate of traditional small Highland stills was high. The geography of Arran made it ideally positioned to benefit from the ill-advised excise reforms of the late 18th century. Within a few years, Arran whisky manufacture had developed into a lucrative business for islanders who were willing to take extraordinary risks, and operate outwith the law.

3

THE ARRAN SMUGGLING NETWORK

THE ILLICIT ECONOMY OF ARRAN was well established by the late 18th century. For over a century, the smuggling of untaxed goods had been widely practised along the island's coastline. The nature of taxation during this period was the predominant reason for the extensive smuggling practices on Arran, and throughout the whole of the United Kingdom. Excise duty was imposed on a host of everyday goods including: beer, bricks, candles, coal, coffee, fish, glass, hops, kelp, leather, malt, paper, salt, soap, sugar, tea, timber, tobacco, vinegar, wine, and wool.[1] Essentially, almost every commodity of value that had an impact on daily life had some form of duty imposed upon it.

Duty was also placed on goods imported from abroad. The British policy of free trade was not widely upheld until the 1840s, consequently, in the 18th century every port and harbour of significance had a permanent Customs House charged with ensuring the collection of duty. Inevitably it was profitable to evade the payment of these taxes and, as the government gradually increased rates throughout the 18th century, avoidance and smuggling became common practice. It was remarked by the novelist Sir Walter Scott that, 'Smuggling was almost universal in Scotland ... for people unaccustomed to imposts and regarding them as an unjust aggression upon their ancient liberties, made no scruple to elude them whenever it was possible to do so.'[2]

Arran was a hotspot for the illegal trafficking of foreign goods during this period due to its prime geographic position and relative isolation. Goods were landed on the coast having been purchased from passing vessels sailing into the western ports of Scotland from the Americas, Ireland and Continental Europe. Islanders would then run these goods across to the mainland in smaller vessels. Here they re-sold the contraband without having to pay burdensome duties, earning themselves a significant profit. The Excise Collector at Rothesay detailed Arran's role in this illicit trade: 'Ships when coming into the Clyde from foreign parts were in use of smuggling ashore at or about the south-east point of the Island of Arran ...'.[3]

The earliest documented smuggling incident relating to Arran occurred in 1671. On 27 April, an Irish vessel landed at Lamlash with a cargo of untaxed goods. The contraband was seized by an armed party, led by the Kilbride minister, Archibald Beith. During the seizure the smugglers forcibly retrieved the goods and set sail for the mainland. Revd Beith and his party pursued them and opened fire, killing two of the crew, one of whom was Allan Gardiner, a merchant from Irvine. Historian William MacKenzie supposed that during the seizure Beith, 'distinguished himself in a most unpastorlike manner.'[4] Given the outcome, this would seem something of an understatement. As a punishment for the severity of his actions the 'militant minister' was tried at the High Court in Edinburgh and was sentenced to be hanged. He was subsequently reprieved and saw out the rest of his life in disgrace, latterly soliciting the Town Council of Rothesay for help and liberty to beg for a living. Beith has since become an infamous figure in the history of Arran's religious leaders, and was dubbed, 'Beith of Kilbride, the reverend slayer,' by MacKenzie in the early 20th century.[5]

Clearly, smuggling in and around Arran was a dangerous occupation. It would however, take more than a murdering minister to deter islanders from this increasingly profitable practice. Nonetheless, some islanders paid a heavy price for their foolhardiness. In 1753, three Arran men were tried for obstructing customs officers at Lamlash. The men involved, James McKirdy, Thomas Hamilton and Alexander Hamilton, were found guilty and sentenced to, 'be banished during their lives to one or other of His Majesty's Plantations in America, never to return to Scotland under pain of being whipped through the streets of Edinburgh by the Common Hangman, and to be banished again ...'.[6] The harshness of the sentence reveals the grim fate facing those caught transporting untaxed goods.

Unperturbed, and driven by increasingly profitable circumstances, smugglers continued to operate on a significant scale in Arran waters. In the early days of smuggling, salt was the main foreign product trafficked by islanders and a great deal was shipped from Ireland to supply the west-coast fishing industry which relied heavily on salt as a preservative. This vital commodity was first taxed in 1702. By 1798 duty had risen to 5 shillings a bushel (approximately 25kg), increasing to the exorbitant figure of 15 shillings per bushel in the early 1800s. This increase made salt-smuggling a very attractive proposition. In 1799, seven salt boats were seized off the south coast of Arran.[7] In 1807, John and Allister Stewart of Whiting Bay were caught smuggling 30 bags, containing 28 bushels (approximately 700kg) of Irish salt, in a small boat four miles off the Kintyre coast.[8]

As smuggling around Arran's shores increased, a concerted effort was mounted by excise officials to suppress the activity. Revenue Cutters regularly patrolled the Firth of Clyde and the North Channel. There were frequent clashes between smugglers and the 'cuttermen', occasionally with tragic consequences. In 1796, a young smuggler was fatally wounded in a vessel conveying salt off the south coast of Arran. The deadly incident was documented in the *Edinburgh Advertiser.*

> On Wednesday evening a young man was shot in a salt boat between the Isles of Pladda and Arran, by a boat's crew belonging to Captain Dowie, of the *Prince Augustus Frederick*, Revenue Cutter. The crew of the smuggling boat having with their oars opposed that of the Revenue's boat making a seizure of it. It is to be lamented that the poor people on the coast should persevere in a trade which by the laws of our country subjects their property to seizure, and exposes their lives to destruction if they make any opposition to the officers of the Revenue – There have of late years been several instances, where the lives of these unfortunate persons have been sacrificed when attempting a feeble resistance to preserve a few bolls of salt.[9]

Salt was not the only untaxed commodity traded by Arran smugglers; they were known to transport all manner of foreign spirits. In 1750, a local boat was seized with 120 casks of rum and brandy, along with two hogsheads of wine. In 1808, Robert McGregor, an Arran excise officer, seized, '2 casks containing 20 gallons foreign rum,' in the possession of Donald Jamison residing at Drimlabarra, near Kildonan.[10] The seized casks were later sold by the Excise at auction, fetching the substantial sum of £11 5s 6d. Arran smugglers were also involved in the running of gunpowder to Ireland. In November 1807, Daniel Currie of Sliddery and Peter McKinnon of Corriecravie were implicated in the landing of 10 casks of powder at Kintyre.[11] The cargo was discovered, 'concealed in Crates Cleaned out as Earthenware …'.[12] It was asserted that the illegal cargo was landed on Arran by an Irish vessel, the *Pricilla* of Ballycastle, on her return voyage to her native land from Glasgow, in order to have a greater chance of avoiding detection. From here it was shipped firstly to Kintyre, and then onto its final destination, the north-east coast of Ireland. Unfortunately for Currie, McKinnon and their smuggling associates, it was discovered by excise officers from Campbeltown.

The Arran smuggling industry certainly exploded in the late 18th and early 19th centuries. This illicit trade was extensive and

well organised, with vast quantities of valuable goods being transported to and from the island without the knowledge of the
Excise. The scale of smuggling activities was so great that during
a plague scare on the island in 1770, the island factor John Burrel
feared that a quarantine imposed by him would be breached by
two or three hundred young men, 'who have no visible means of
making bread but by smuggling ...'.[13] This considerable smuggling network was able to facilitate the transportation of Arran
whisky, as its popularity and profitability grew in the late 1700s.
MacKenzie states that there were, 'two sides to the smuggling
business; introducing stuff which had escaped duty, and the
manufacture of whisky under illegal conditions, which therefore
again had to be sold clandestinely.'[14] By the early 1800s whisky
became the chief commodity transported by Arran smugglers as
illicit distillation grew to unprecedented levels.

4

THE RISE OF
ILLICIT DISTILLING

I N THE LATE 18th century the Arran factor, William Murray, lamented, 'No notice of Arran at this time is possible without a reference to the making of the famous "Arran water".'[1] MacBride, writing in the early 1900s, argued that illicit distillation was at its height in 1797. He refers to a letter from Arran during this period describing whisky as a, 'perfect drug in the market – it being supposed that there were no less than 50 stills at the south end of the island.'[2]

The Kilmory minister, Angus McMillan, also documented the scale of illicit distilling in the southern district[3] throughout the early 19th century, suggesting, 'there being few, if any, in the parish, who, at some period of their lives, were not engaged in some department of smuggling.'[4] It would appear that unlicensed distilling thrived in the relative isolation of Kilmory, which incorporated the southern and western regions. South-end residents developed a reputation for 'lawlessness' during this period. The Hamilton estate factor Robert Brown, attributed this to, 'their intercourse with the Irish, and likewise smuggling into the low country.'[5] It was stated by Brown that, 'in the north end of the island the people do not smuggle; at least they smuggle very little ...'.[6] Whilst illicit distilling was concentrated to the south and west of the island, it was not exclusively practised in these localities. In 1802, 41 Arran tenants were summonsed to the Rothesay Excise Court, 29 residents facing charges related to illicit activities, and 12 to give evidence; all of the accused resided in Arran's northern and eastern districts.[7]

Clearly Arran was becoming a growing problem for the excise administration with its limited manpower and resources. The Collector at Rothesay wrote to the Excise Board in Edinburgh, declaring that, 'A great number of Inhabitants of Arran occupy themselves; extensively in practices inimical to the Interests of the Revenue ... their efforts are all in illicit malting and distilling ...'.[8] Excise officers were also hindered in their tasks by colluding informants. Distilling and smuggling were shared activities, with nearly all members of the island society involved in one way or another. Local knowledge allowed signals and messages to be passed between communities, giving distillers time to hide incriminating evidence. The extent and sophistication of this system was documented in the correspondence between Mr MacLeod Bannatyne, of the Customs and Excise Board, and the Arran factor, William Stevenson:

> It appears to me that your islanders being so closely connected with each other and so generally interacted in protecting offenders that nothing is likely to be effected by sending an officer and party to Brodick or Lamlash, because they are no sooner arrived than their objective comes to be known, and intelligence will of course be conveyed to the persons meant to be seized, long before the party can reach their places of residence ...[9]

The communal nature of illicit distilling and the infrastructure in place to ensure its success, initially made it difficult for the Excise to detect and prosecute those involved. In order to establish some sort of control and regain order over the islanders, Stevenson requested that a party of 20 military men be stationed on the island. His request was accepted and in the early 1800s it was detailed that on Arran, 'some soldiers are usually stationed ... to assist the Excise Officers.'[10] The local excise gaugers were clearly overwhelmed by the scale of illegal distillation.

With military support, excise officers gradually asserted some jurisdiction over Arran, making a considerable number of seizures in the first decade of the 19th century. In 1801, the *Glasgow Courier* reported that:

> Mr James Craig, Supervisor of the Excise here, and two of his officers Alexander Williamson and Wm McLean, accompanied by a party of the 10th or Edinburgh Militia, sailed from this port [*Ayr*] on board the *Prince Augustus Frederick*, Revenue Cutter, with Captain Dowie, for the island of Arran, where they discovered seven private distilleries, five private malsters [*sic*], and seized three large stills, which Mr Craig has lodged in the Excise Office here.[11]

Four years later in July 1805, two small casks of whisky were seized by James McBride, tidewaiter, on the north shore of Brodick.[12] The whisky was confiscated from James Lamont and an unnamed local companion, 'under the clouds of night.'[13] Rather than resisting the seizure the islanders humbly accepted their fate and helped carry the casks, 'on their backs ... to William Hendry's house being a distance of about three quarters of a mile ...'.[14] Lamont and his smuggling associate were paid the sum of four shillings and sixpence for their assistance. Given the circumstances the exciseman was, 'well pleased to get Lamont to carry the whiskie for the agreed [payment] ...'.[15] This incident reveals an unusual demonstration of mutual understanding between the gaugers and smugglers; a rare occurrence on Arran in the early 1800s.

In 1807, James McGregor, officer of the Excise at Brodick, was violently attacked by a smuggler, 'when walking the Highway from Lagg to Benecargan.' McGregor had observed a man leading a horse and cart, carrying two wooden casks. Believing that the casks contained, 'smuggled or contraband aquavitae', he attempted to secure the cart in the name of the Excise. His action was met with considerable resistance, and the smuggler, 'violently seized the said James McGregor by the Collar, and threatened to knock him down with a bludgeon ... which he held in his hand.' In the ensuing scuffle, McGregor was kicked so severely that his leg was broken, 'about three inches below the knee.'[16] As a result, he was forced to abandon the seizure and the smuggler rode off with the contraband, leaving the stricken officer in agony at the roadside. Daniel Cook, sub-tenant of Benecarigan (Bennecarrigan) farm was accused of the assault and tried before the Circuit Court at Inveraray. A verdict of 'not proven' was delivered as it was deemed there was insufficient evidence to form 'complete proof' of Cook's involvement. Nevertheless, McGregor, 'swore positively to MacCook as being the person who deforced him and broke his leg.'[17] Whoever the perpetrator, it would appear that they had a fortunate escape from justice. It was noted in the aftermath of the court proceedings that, 'the trial will have good effect in discouraging the Arran people from commission of similar outrages.'[18] This was a rather optimistic prediction and the apparent foresight was certainly misjudged.

Clashes between island smugglers and excisemen were becoming increasingly common on Arran, as officers attempted to suppress widespread illicit distilling. Once more in 1807, south-end tenants were suspected of outrages against the gaugers. Alexander Stewart of Largiemenoch (Largymeanoch), south of Whiting Bay, was accused of assaulting, beating and violently maltreating John Hamilton, officer of the Excise residing at Millhill near Lamlash. It was reputed that Hamilton:

> having reason to believe that Donald Stewart Farmer in Largiemenoch, father of the said Alexander Stewart, was employed in distilling aqua-vitae contrary to law attempted in discharge of his duty to enter the house of Donald Stewart where the operation was going on ... when about to enter the said house he was met by Alexander Stewart who struck him violently with his fist, tore part of his clothes and swore that he would put John Hamilton to death if he ever ventured to come near his fathers' house again ...[19]

Unperturbed by the threats and determined to complete what would have been a valuable seizure, Hamilton unwisely returned to the area a few days later, supported by his son Robert. The pair detected an active illicit still in a house on the farm of Largiebeg (Largybeg), but were once again barred from entering the dwelling by the local distillers. Having destroyed a quantity of wash that was in casks by the side of the house, the exciseman and his son retreated from the settlement. During this they were ambushed by Alexander Stewart, accompanied by his brother Robert. It was alleged that Stewart violently attacked John Hamilton landing serval blows to his head with a bludgeon. Fortunately for the pair, they were rescued by the assistance of John Cumming, herdsman at Largiebeg, who sheltered them in his small dwelling. Here the Stewarts renewed their attack, desperately attempting to force open the bolted door, 'with the felonious purpose of murdering the said John Hamilton and his assistant ... Alexander Stewart being armed with an open knife ...'.[20] Despite the efforts of the Stewart brothers, latterly assisted by three other unidentified islanders, the door remained intact and they desisted their attack, enabling the wounded and shaken exciseman and his son to flee to the safety of Lamlash.

Several months later Stewart was summonsed to attend the Inveraray Circuit Court to answer to the aforementioned crimes. Having failed to appear he was subsequently outlawed and declared a fugitive. Two years later, in May 1809, Stewart appeared before John Blaine, the Sheriff Substitute of Rothesay, claiming that he did not receive his court summons as he, 'had gone to serve a farmer in Ayrshire during the Harvest' and was, 'at that time residing with one John Baird in the neighbourhood of Maybole.'[21]

Despite his pleas of innocence and his supposed ignorance of being declared an outlaw, Stewart was incarcerated in the

Tolbooth of Rothesay and tried at Inveraray in October 1809. Here the court heard Stewart's declaration which contradicted Hamilton's version of events. The accused smuggler claimed that in the first instance he did not assault Hamilton at Largiemenoch. He did see the exciseman at the nearby settlement of Largiemore (Largymore), but as far as Stewart was aware there, 'was no distilling going on at that place.'[22] Stewart further mentioned that he was not present when the Excise officer and his son had attempted to carry out the subsequent seizure at Largiebeg. He did, however, briefly come across the pair while waiting to meet with his brother near the house of John Cumming. Stewart positively asserted that he spent less than three minutes in the neighbourhood, amusing himself by whittling a piece of wood, and that neither he or his brother threatened the excisemen or attempted to enter the nearby steading.

Unlike the Rothesay Sheriff Substitute, the assembled jury, consisting of a number of south-end natives, was sympathetic to the accused smuggler, finding Alexander Stewart 'not guilty' of outrages against John and Robert Hamilton. The exoneration of both Cook and Stewart, certainly demonstrates that during the first decade of 19th century the local courts were favourable to Arran's illicit distillers.

Despite the numerous setbacks and threats of violence, Excise officers continued to carry out their duties with a degree of diligence. A Petition letter dated 1806, from several residents of Torlin (Torrylinn), Sliddery, and Bennecarrigan, states that the defendants, 'like many others in the Island of Arran, are accused by your Honour's Officers of having transgressed against the Laws of Excise ...'.[23] The correspondence highlights the active work of the officers throughout the island as they attempted to curtail illicit practices. Local excisemen carried out a number of successful seizures, most notably in 1807 as reported by the *Glasgow Herald*: 'A few days ago, Messrs McNair and McLaren, officers of excise in Arran, seized and destroyed 1,100 gallons of wash in a private distillery, carried on in a cove on the shore of Torrmore in that island.'[24] This was a substantial capture, revealing that the stationing of excisemen on the island was effective in checking some of the illicit manufacture.

In September 1807, a small quantity of wash was found on John Robertson's premises, at Torbeg. Robertson appealed to William Stevenson, the island factor to exonerate him of guilt, declaring, 'your Petitioner is sensible of the immorality of making grain into malt and there upon distilling whisky ...'.[25] Robertson further testified that his own son was guilty of the misdemeanour, having been convicted of illicit distillation on an earlier occasion. This was a highly unusual incident. By incriminating his own son, Robertson was defying traditional Highland values. Perhaps he supposed that the factor would be sympathetic to his son's plight, or he had finally grown tired of these illicit antics and was unwilling to take the blame. In any case, the actions of Robertson defied convention and he risked incurring the wrath, not only of his son, but of the wider community. It was common for islanders accused of informing against their neighbours to fervently deny the accusations. In December 1805, Neil Shaw went as far as petitioning the Kilmory Kirk Session to refute allegations against his reputation:

> Neil Shaw in Burican reports to the Session that the families of Iver Cook and Archibald MacNeil in said farm Calumniate his character by saying to others and also to himself that he informed the Excise men against them, and was the cause of subjecting them to a fine. After loud discussion it was understood, as far as could be traced out that Neil Shaw was innocent of said charges he and said antagonists were enjoined to forget all and be at peace, which they [agreed] to and shook hands ...[26]

Intriguingly, at no point during proceedings did the Kirk Session reprimand those found guilty of illicit distillation. The session merely settled the dispute regarding Shaw's reputation. This strongly suggests the widespread acceptance of private distilling, even amongst the island's religious leaders. In fact some Arran ministers were directly involved in whisky-smuggling activities. It was recorded in the memoir of Revd John MacAlister, Free Church minister at Brodick in the 1840s, that he took part in smuggling as a young man growing up on the small farm of Kilpatrick on the island's west coast.[27] His smuggling endeavours were, however, undertaken out of necessity in order to support his widowed mother, long before he received his calling from God.

Another case of informing occurred in 1807. This time William Stewart (Stuart) of Bennecarrigan wrote a letter asking for assistance from the factor, James Lamont:

> That Peter MacLeran Officer of Excise in company with some of the Military men now stationed in this Island ... seized a ... quantity of Malt in the Miln of Torrylin, and that several persons in the farm of Benicarigan makes use of your petitioners name as being the informer of said malt to the Revenue Officers or Kings men – your petitioner being desirous to clear himself of the above calamity ... [is] willing to make oath before your Honour that he never informed any Excise Officer or Kings men of any malt or seizure of any kind made by them.[28]

The drastic measures that Shaw and Stewart were willing take, shows that informers were almost as loathed as the excise officers. It was documented by the Arran factor in the 1820s that James McCurdy of Ballymeanoch was, 'an informer and hated by his neighbours.'[29] Clearly there was no greater dishonour than betraying your fellow islanders. The battle lines had been drawn: distillers on one side defending what they considered their birthright, against agents of the Excise who threatened it. The incident documented by Stewart also highlights the escalating violence between the opposing parties as excisemen became increasingly reliant on military assistance for their own protection.

Arran factors were also getting drawn into excise disputes. Factors acted as Justices of the Peace for the island, appointed by the main proprietor, the Duke of Hamilton. It was therefore the responsibility of these principle land agents, to maintain law and order throughout Arran. This included dealing with the growing problem of illicit distilling. Island factors, however had a vested interest in this issue. Clandestine distilling and smuggling provided a ready market for island grain, maintaining a steady income stream, ensuring tenants were able to pay rent to the Hamilton estate. Gavin D. Smith, in his work *The Secret Still*, suggests that a proportion of the island rent was directly paid in whisky, 'which was collected at Brodick and then smuggled across to the mainland.'[30] Smith also claims that the factor, Robert Brown, was heavily involved in this illegal shipment of whisky. Unfortunately, he does not reveal the primary source of this information, and the direct involvement of Brown seems unlikely as he was responsible for implementing tough measures to combat illicit distilling from 1815 onwards (see Chapter 11). Nonetheless, it is apparent that some of Brown's predecessors were sympathetic to known unlicensed distillers. Many cases were dropped and nominal fines imposed. This leniency is apparent in a letter dated 1809, from the tacksmen of Bennecarrigan to the factor, James Lamont:

> We are greatly obliged to your Honour for your advice to us because there is no other man to look after us but your honour and we the undermentioned persons are willing to pay for the agent to the outmost according to your discretion to us this is the name of us that was found guilty by the Excisemen in the farm of Benecarigan, James Nicoll, Archibald Cook, Malcolm Cook, Neil Curry, Donald Cook, Donald McLarty Jun., Neill Cook, Duncan McKinnon, and we are

willing to do any thing that your Honour will bid us to do because we
depend on your honour to assistance us.[31]

This pleading correspondence clearly shows that island tenants
reasoned that Lamont would be willing to assist them in regard
to accusations of illicit distillation. In 1809, Lamont certainly
displayed a degree of compassion for the plight facing accused
distillers. He requested that Excise Courts be held on Arran
rather than at Rothesay as the additional travel was an, 'inconve-
nience to the poor people by absenting themselves from their
homes and families ...'.[32] There is little doubt that Lamont and
other Arran agents initially displayed clemency in their approach
to unlicensed distilling. Personal interests formed the basis of
these actions. Certainly, Lamont and his contemporaries were
well aware of the scale of illicit activities and the dangers faced by
excise officials to limit these practices. In the face of economic
benefits however, it was more prudent to turn a blind eye than to
actively intervene and suppress illicit distillation.

5

THE WHISKY MAKERS

'What could the Arran folk dae wi their baurley gin
they didna mak whisky o't?'[1]

IN THE EARLY 19th century, Robert Brown suggested that
illicit distilling on Arran was carried out by, 'the rank of the
lowest tenants.'[2] Certainly, the manufacture of untaxed
whisky on the island was predominately carried out by subsistence farmers and cottars.[3] The court declaration of Neil Cook,
who was accused of attacking an exciseman in 1807, provides a
vital insight into the circumstances of those undertaking small-
scale whisky manufacture:

> ... he was not brought up to any particular profession but has wrought
> at times as a Labourer and as a Ploughman and upon one occasion he
> went to the North Highlands to fish for Herrings ... he possesses the
> twenty fourth part of the farm of Benecargan his part thereof
> consisting of a horse gang for which he pays about six pounds of rent
> yearly declares that he is married and has four children and he, his wife
> and family all subsist upon the produce of that farm ... declares That he
> has been in the practise of distilling part of the Bear which has been
> raised upon his own possession, but he has not been in use of
> purchasing any bear for that purpose.[4]

The testimony of a self-confessed illicit distiller further demonstrates that whisky manufacture formed a key part of the
substance economy of Arran. Illegal whisky production allowed
tenants to fully utilise the arable produce of their small farm
holdings, providing vital additional revenue. When asked why
illicit distilling persisted on Arran, the exciseman Robert Stewart
remarked, 'On the account of there being so many small farmers

with a quantity of bere or barley, and I suppose they think it will pay better to distil it into whisky.'[5]

Evidently, illicit distillers were motivated by financial circumstances. Many economically vulnerable tenants were tempted to engage in illicit distilling as it enabled them to pay their ever-increasing rents, providing them with a degree of security. For many of the island's widows, the infirm and elderly, small-scale distilling was the only means of employment and income. The 1806 petition of John Murphie documents the direct involvement of widows in Arran production:

> ... lately a poor woman Widow Wylie ... having a small quantity of malt to manufacture to make up her rent, used the freedom to put her distilling utensils into a new house built by your petitioner which was without doors or windows … without asking his liberty. That she herself confesses the fact, and is willing (tho' poor) to fund to the damage ...[6]

The manufacture of whisky was clearly a cash-incentivised enterprise largely carried out by the poorest class of tenants. Distilling was one of the few occupations available to this vulnerable class, ensuring their continued survival on the island. The importance of this illegal enterprise to these tenants is further documented in a letter from John McCurdy, East Bennan, to James Lamont, dated 1808:

> That your Petitioner is reduced by Infirmity and old age, so as he is not able to help himself or family for six years past ... and has none to take care of him in his old age, but a little Boy, and a little Girl ... that this morning Mr Stuart the Exciseman came to your petr. house, where the produce of the year was manufactured to Coachan[7] by a borrowed still ...[8]

McCurdy further lamented that the seizure made it difficult for him to pay his rent, in addition to the wages of his two servants and the fine imposed upon him by the Excise. The plight of the aged McCurdy reveals the importance of distilling to islanders and the risks involved. Many small tenants would invest their entire annual grain harvest in distilling ventures. If detected, they were left with nothing. It is little surprise that the excisemen were so despised on Arran as they threatened the islanders very existence. Many vulnerable tenants, like McCurdy, simply could not afford to fail.

Murphie and McCurdy's declarations also emphasise the important role women played in distilling ventures. Whisky-making was often viewed as an extension of women's domestic duties. It was stated by Thomas Pennant, when documenting his tour of Scotland in 1772, that women made whisky while their husbands were at work in the fields. Robert Brown noted that in neighbouring Argyllshire, it was common for respectable would-be distillers to, 'delegate it to servant maids and inferior people to carry on the process of illicit distillation, so that the principal may escape detection.'[9] He was however, uncertain if this practice extended to Arran. Undoubtedly, island women of all ages were occupied in distilling activities. In 1802, five Arran women were summoned to the Excise Court in Rothesay, accused of involvement in unlicensed manufacture.

It must be noted, however, that illicit manufacture was not exclusively conducted by the poorest members of the island community. The petition of the tacksmen of Bennecarrigan (see page 31) documents the direct involvement of more respectable members of Arran society. As alluded to in Chapter 2, tacksmen were important figures in pre-Clearances Highland culture, belonging to a higher-ranking social group. Dr Samuel Johnson perhaps most aptly defined the standing of this influential set suggesting that, 'Next in dignity to the Laird is the Tacksman; a large taker or leaseholder of land, of which he keeps part, as a domain, in his own hand, and lets part to under tenants.'[10] On Lewis it was documented that reputable tacksmen used their authority to allocate grain to their subtenants for explicit use in illicit distillation. The whisky produced was subsequently sold in mainland markets earning the tacksman and the wider community a considerable profit. From the implication of the Bennecarigan tacksmen in clandestine manufacture it could be argued that this practice was also common on Arran. In fact, their detection by Excise officers in 1809 suggests that the south-end 'gentry',[11] on occasion, adopted a more hands-on approach than their Outer Hebridean and Kintyre counterparts in regards to unlicensed whisky production.

Nonetheless, it was the poorest class of tenants who, for the most part, ran the greatest risks of illicit whisky distilling. It provided women and other economically vulnerable islanders with a critical source of cash income during the early 19th century. The importance of the trade to the fragile Arran economy during this period was revealed in the testimony of an aged islander interviewed by MacKenzie in the early 20th century. He remarked that, 'whisky and kelp were the only two ways people made their money.'[12] There is little doubt that whisky-making was of incalculable importance to many islanders. Women, alongside poor and elderly tenants were heavily reliant on the industry as the main participants in 'peatreek' manufacture. Illicit distilling flourished throughout Arran, aided in part by the sympathetic attitudes of the ruling class, support of the island tacksmen, and the ineffectiveness of central Excise policy. Unlicensed whisky-making was a widely accepted part of island life, becoming central to the subsistence Arran economy in the late 18th and early 19th centuries.

6

EARLY LEGAL DISTILLING
ON ARRAN

A LTHOUGH ILLICIT WHISKY PRODUCTION and
smuggling flourished during this period, legal distilling
was also carried out intermittently on the island in the
1790s. John Hamilton, the minister of Kilmory, documented in
1793 that, '3 licensed distilleries have lately been erected in the
island, which will exhaust a great part of the barley that can
henceforth be spared.'[1] Confirmation of this can be found in the
correspondence between William Stevenson and the Excise
Collector at Ayr, where he states that, 'there are three inland
Distilleries in the Island of 40 Gallons each ...'.[2] These legal
ventures operated on a very small scale. This was the maximum
still size permitted for legal distillation in Highland regions as set
out by amendments to the 1784 Wash Act. As a result, the
capacity of these licensed ventures was not much larger than the
bothy stills operated by illicit distillers.[3]

Government intervention helped stimulate licensed production in Scotland. The volume of spirits charged with duty doubled
in the year following the passing of the Wash Act. By lowering the
annual licence fee and the duty rates, the new legislation partially
encouraged small-scale legal distilling in Highland regions.
Distillers in the north were given preferential treatment over their
Lowland competitors in an attempt to stamp out growing illicit
distilling and smuggling. These amendments to the distilling laws
undoubtedly encouraged the establishment of early legal ventures
throughout the Highlands, including on Arran.

The first licensed Arran distillery was located at Glenshant. This settlement was cleared in 1852, when the 'old' village of Brodick and its surrounding clachans were demolished on the 11th duke's orders, to make way for the expansion of the castle pleasure grounds. James C Inglis, writing in the 1930s, lamented that the settlements of, 'Mossend, Drum-a-clarey, the old Wool Mill, Glenshant, Cladach, Dykehead, the Cnocans, high and low, were all swept into oblivion, and now there are practically no traces of such hamlets having existed, except some old landmarks here and there, known only to a few.'[4] Inglis further detailed that long-forgotten Glenshant was, 'practically part of the entrance to Glen Rosa.'[5] A rough plan from c.1800 depicts its location to the east of Glen Rosa, on the opposite bank of the Glen Rosa Water, roughly situated at NS 005377. The destruction of Glenshant in the 19th century makes it difficult to establish the site of the legal distillery. A wool mill was marked on the c.1800 plan, and its ruined foundations remain visible on the banks of the Cnocan Burn (NS 00643776). It could be argued that the distillery building was repurposed following its closure in the 1790s to facilitate the mill. Unfortunately, there is no documentary evidence to back up this supposition and the exact location of Glenshant Distillery remains a mystery.

Nonetheless, a document titled, *Account of sundrie articles and utensils and other adornments made by Alexander McLean, for the use of Glenshant Distillery from 1 Dec 1790 to 1 Jan 1793*, uncovered in the Arran Estate Office, provides a vital insight into the workings of this early Arran venture. The distillery was established in 1790 by Alexander McLean, with John McLean acting as the manager of the business. Equipment and apparatus was sourced from Saltcoats and Kintyre, with a still and boiler manufactured and transported from Campbeltown at a cost of £11 10s. Over the course of two years a maltster was employed at the distillery earning an annual salary of £15. Peggy Donaldson was employed as the brewer at Glenshant, earning an annual wage of £13. As previously outlined, it was customary for women to be involved in illicit whisky production and this must have extended to early legal distilling on Arran, as Peggy held a key role in the Glenshant operation. The whisky distilled was transported to Lamlash, Corrie and Lochranza by Archibald McBride and Malcolm McMillan, so the distillate was predominately sold in the local Arran market. The total operating costs of the distillery over the three-year period amounted to £91 8s 10d. Intriguingly, William Stevenson, the Arran factor, contributed £42 13s 10d towards the bill, suggesting that either he, or the Hamilton family, held a substantial stake in the business and were directly supporting the distillery. During this period, notable landowners were heavily involved in legal distilling in other regions of the Highlands and Islands. On Tiree in the 1790s, the Duke of Argyll constructed two legal distilleries in an attempt to curtail widely practised illicit production.[6]

Another of the early Arran distilleries was located at the Whitehouse in Lamlash, established by James and Peter McBride. A letter uncovered in the Arran Estate office, from the McBrides to Captain James Hamilton, documents their intention to establish a legal still: 'As we are desirous of carrying on a Whisky Distillery at Lamlash we expect will tend to your and our advantage, and as you are prepossessed of a proper Malting Kiln with other amenities which would answer our purpose.'[7] The McBride's subsequently obtained a 10-year lease in 1793 of the Malting Kiln and a small square acre of land, 'on the Whitehouse parks', from Captain Hamilton who was the commander of the *Prince William Henry* Revenue Cutter, which cruised the waters of the Firth of Clyde attempting to combat smuggling activities. No doubt Hamilton would have kept a close eye on the goings-on at the Whitehouse distillery. It was documented that the annual rent for the property was set at £10. A 'proper still house' was to be built on the square acre of land adjacent to the Malting Kiln at the McBride's expense, provided Captain Hamilton diverted water from the nearby kirk ground, 'to be enclosed by a depth of wall.'[8]

From this correspondence the location of the Whitehouse distillery can be established. Evidently, the distillery formed part of the kiln and corn mill site, situated on the ground between Park Terrace and the now demolished Whitehouse Hotel (NS 02453097). Unfortunately, in 2005 the ruined mill buildings were also pulled down and modern housing was built on the site. A standing building, recording and watching brief was conducted by Rathmell Archaeology prior to and during demolition. They ascertained from their archaeological surveys and examination of historical documentation that the site was originally a corn-drying kiln.[9] In 1717, a corn mill had been constructed, incorporating the existing kiln structure.[10] The McBride's letter to Captain Hamilton reveals that a building housing a legal still was integrated into this existing mill and kiln site in 1793. It is likely that the buildings fell into a state of disrepair not long after the distillery ceased production in 1797, as the mill site is marked as a ruin on the 1st edition Ordnance Survey Map from 1864.

In September 1793, a still, worm and stand were sent by Robert MacGrigor from Campbeltown, via Iain Shaw of Kilpatrick for use in the newly constructed distillery. A letter between the two parties reveals that MacGrigor was also involved in financing the distillery:

> I have also sent you Twenty pounds which you will be so good as [to] acknowledge upon receipt if you find this sum not competent let me know, I shall accommodate you with a little more – I engaged a man for you for six months at six pounds who will act as Distiller and Maltman with a little assistance ... The amount of your utensils from this amounts to nearly Ten pounds I hope you will receive all in good order.[11]

Although supplied with specialist equipment from the mainland, the distillery did make use of locally sourced raw materials. Between December 1794 and December 1795, the cost of purchasing these resources amounted to £112 6s[12] and locally grown bere barley accounted for the majority of this expense. All of this vital raw ingredient was purchased from farms located within the parish of Kilbride as the Wash Act stipulated that only grain grown in the parish in which the distillery was located could be used in whisky production. The purchasing of vast quantities of barely suggests that the McBrides were not directly involved in agriculture. Noted whisky historians, Michael Moss and John Hume, suggested that Highland distilleries of this period were mostly owned by local farmers and tradesmen.[13] It appears that the proprietors of the Whitehouse distillery were the latter. Peat was also purchased for the distillery which would have fuelled the still and the nearby kiln used to dry grain prior to its use. It was argued by Lowland distillers that this fuel source gave legal producers in Kintyre, Bute, Arran and Cowal an unfair advantage over them:

> ... the Highland Distiller uses a considerable Proportion of Peat and Wood Fuel, which he gets almost at his own Door, and at a trifling Expense, and which gives his Spirits that peculiar Flavour that so many People are fond of, and which gives them a decided Preference in the Lowland Market.[14]

The use of peat would have certainly affected the character of the whisky. It is highly likely that the legal Arran distilleries would have been producing whisky in the traditional manner, similar to illicit producers, using pot stills, weak washes, and distilling at a much slower rate than their Lowland competitors. This would have produced a flavoursome whisky of a much higher quality. Lowland whisky was often compromised by the use of unmalted grain and the adoption of rapid distillation methods.

MacKenzie MacBride, writing in 1911, revealed further details regarding the Whitehouse distillery, suggesting that, 'in the grounds of the Whitehouse, there was a licensed still of the capacity of forty gallons ... from December 1793 to November 1794, whisky was sold to the amount of £500 at 2s. per Scotch pint, or 4s. per gallon.'[15] This secondary account coupled with the personal correspondence of the McBrides, provides us with a clear picture of the characteristics of the Whitehouse distillery. This legal venture was very small, producing approximately 1,500 gallons of whisky annually. The average output of a legal Highland distillery during this period was between 1,000 and 2,000 gallons per year. Furthermore, it is apparent that the owners of the venture, the McBrides, did not possess sufficient nous or capital to establish a successful distilling business. They required a considerable degree of outside assistance to source the relevant expertise and investment at the outset of the venture.

This was a problem for a considerable number of legal distill-eries in Highland areas, and many struggled financially during the final decade of the 18th century. Their economic vulnerability was exposed by duty increases which made legal distilling on a small scale virtually impossible. Between 1793 and 1797, duty was raised from £1 10s per gallon of still content to £6 10s.[16] Furthermore in 1797, at the insistence of the large Lowland distillers, an Intermediate District between the Highland and Lowland excise areas was established with duty levied at £9. Arran was included in this new area, as shown on the map in the plate section. This had significant negative implications for legal distilling in the region. Many new distilleries simply went out of business. The McBrides noted the precarious nature of taking up a distilling licence in the 1790s, stating that, 'if there shall happen to be any alteration in the Distillery Law said we shall have it in our opinion to give up the works ...'.[17] This foresight proved to be correct, and the duty rises of 1797 played a significant role in the demise of the Whitehouse distillery, and the other legal ventures on Arran.

The location of the third Arran distillery from the 1790s remains unknown. Glenshant and Whitehouse were both located within the parish of Kilbride and the legislation outlined in the Wash Act stipulated that no more than two legal distilleries were permitted in each parish in Highland areas. Therefore the third legal still must have been situated somewhere in the parish of Kilmory. The settlement of Lagg would seem the most likely location as a licensed distillery was established here in the 1820s (see Chapter 15). Unfortunately, there is no conclusive documentary evidence to confirm this, or pinpoint an exact location.

Nonetheless, it can be concluded that the three legal stills of the 1790s were short-lived undertakings limited by a lack of capital and amendments to excise legislation. A 40-gallon still capacity and the use of grain grown in the local parish restricted output to approximately 1,500 gallons per annum. The distilleries were established by local residents, the McLeans and the McBrides, who employed specialist maltmen, brewers, and distillers to oversee production as they possessed limited capital and little distilling knowledge. In the case of Whitehouse, cash resources were further stretched by the practice of buying in vast quantities of local bere barley. As a result, these small distilleries were highly vulnerable to changing economic and excise conditions. Even the financial assistance of the Hamilton estate at Glenshant could not save legal distilling on the island in the late 18th century.

Critically, these licensed distilleries were prohibited from exporting their produce to neighbouring Lowland districts, most notably Ayrshire. The export of whisky from the Highlands to the Lowlands was outlawed by the distilling legislation of the 1780s. The exclusion from key markets put legal Arran distillers at a considerable disadvantage to their illicit competitors. Illicit distillers benefited greatly from the growing demand for high-quality Highland pot-still whisky in the under-supplied markets of Ayrshire. The introduction of the Intermediate District and the resulting duty increases was the coup de grâce for legal distilling on Arran in the 1790s.

The failure of these ventures mirrored the experience of other distilleries incorporated into this area. It was observed that, 'A few individuals in the intermediate district made trial whether it was possible to carry on the business subject to the £9 duty; but the first quarter convinced them it was altogether out of their powers.'[18] Poorly drafted and ill-considered excise legislation effectively ended early legal distilling on Arran, and provided further stimulus to burgeoning illicit production and smuggling.

7

THE MAKING OF ARRAN
PEATREEK

THE FAILURE OF LEGAL DISTILLING on the island in the late 18th century drove the Arran whisky industry entirely underground. As previously stated, illicit distilling flourished on the island and formed a key part of the island's economy and culture. Illicit Arran whisky enjoyed a fine reputation throughout mainland western Scotland. In 1824, renowned Scottish geologist and traveller, John MacCulloch, remarked 'That of Arran, in the older days, was the Burgundy of all the vintages.'[1] MacCulloch was an associate of Sir Walter Scott, and his comments allude to the prospect of illicit Arran whisky being enjoyed by members of the Scottish social elite. It was further asserted that Arran was, 'particularly famous for the excellence of its fine flavoured whisky.'[2] Undoubtedly, the island's illicit produce was of the highest order. Arran's natural amenities contributed to the first-rate whisky made in its unlicensed stills. *The Scotsman* reported in the 1830s that, 'The acknowledged excellence of the Arran whisky is attributed to the peculiar and admirable quality of the water.'[3] A statement that is as true today as the day it was written.

Undoubtedly, the character of unlicensed Arran whisky was also shaped by those distilling it and the methods and techniques they employed. Islanders carried out this traditional craft with a high degree of skill and pride. Bere (bear) was the main grain used in island whisky production. This four-rowed type of barley was well-suited to the climate of western Scotland, making up half of the Hebridean crop acreage in the early 1800s. Bere ripened between 14 to 21 days earlier than other cereals and required a growing season of only 10 to 15 weeks. The fertile coastline of Arran was perfect for its cultivation. In 1818 the *Farmer's Magazine* reported that on Arran:

> Bear ... is cultivated everywhere; and being the basis of the whiskey manufacture, the people have a warm side to it, and give it a great proportion of the good land, and the best manure ... Some instances there are of ... astonishing crops of bear; particularly as was noticed in the tour, at Whitefarland, on the west coast; I do not think I ever saw better; and so far advanced towards ripening, that I should wonder although it were ready for the sickle before the month August is at an end.[4]

Bere was clearly given preference over other grain crops for the express purpose of distilling. Producing whisky from this raw ingredient required a considerable amount of time-consuming preparation. Firstly, it had to be steeped in water for two to three days in order to trigger germination of the grain. The Arran factor, Robert Brown, documented that this process was carried out, 'in ponds and out of the way places.'[5] It was then spread out and malted in fields or secluded caves on the coast. Brown lamented the distillers use of these rudimentary methods:

> I have seen the process of malting carried on in the open field, that there must be a great destruction of grain. I have seen the grain swelled and trampled in the mud; there must, in my opinion be a great quantity of grain destroyed and lost by illegal distillation.[6]

The malt that was not spoiled during this stage was bagged and transported to a local kiln for drying. Most Arran clachans had communal kilns for drying grain. Several ruined corn-kiln structures were marked at the settlements of Smuraig, Largymore, Margareoch, and Penrioch on the 1864 Ordnance Survey Map.

These kilns were circular constructions, with a conical interior forming part of a drying chamber. A horizontal flue fed heat into the chamber from a peat burning fireplace below. The use of peat in the kilning process would have influenced the characteristics of the whisky, imparting a strong smoky flavour.

After the malt was dried it was ground into a coarse grist. When Robert Bauchop mapped the island between 1807 and 1812, he recorded five estate mills. These would have facilitated this aspect of whisky production. Additionally, small quantities of grain could be ground by hand using querns or husking-stones. Millers operating out of the larger estate mills were certainly implicated in the illicit distilling process. In 1803, Hugh McKenzie, miller at Shedog, in the Shiskine valley, and Hugh Ker, assistant miller at Lochranza, were both fined the considerable sum of £3 3s for failing to appear at the Rothesay Excise Court to testify against their fellow islanders.[7] Apparently, they were unwilling to incriminate their neighbours or themselves in any illicit undertakings. In other regions of the Highlands, including neighbouring Kintyre, millers were often intimidated and coerced into grinding malt for groups of illicit distillers. Unlicensed producers operating at the south-end of Arran utilised the mill at Lagg, which also played a critical role in the formation of a licensed distillery in the region in the 1820s (see Chapter 15). A considerable quantity of malt, belonging to the tenants of Bennecarrigan, was seized in this mill building in 1807. It is highly unlikely that the mill at Brodick was utilised for illicitly processing malt during the first decade of the 19th century, as it was managed by one of the local excise officers.

After milling was carried out, the grist was mixed with hot water to produce a liquid called 'wort', which was then fermented to become 'wash'. Whisky historian SW Sillet gives a detailed outline of how illicit distillers carried out the processes of mashing and fermentation:

Mashing was carried out simply by tipping the dried malt into a cauldron or drum containing hot water, and more often than not, a layer of heather for draining purposes, and heating it up for a couple of hours over a peat fire ... The resulting fermentable worts were then poured or drained into a home-made fermenting vessel, and the process of mashing repeated a second time using fresh water on the original grains ... Mashing occupied the best part of five hours, and on its completion, the smugglers had only to inject a quantity of barm into the fermenting tub before retiring for upwards of two days; that is for the duration of fermentation ...8

John McCulloch documented that on Arran and in other Highland regions, 'wash is manufactured in a rude hut, in some retired or concealed spot, poorly provided with a few casks and tubs.'9 He also explained that, 'the superiority of the Highland spirits arises from the thinness and acidity of the wash, and from the slow manner in which the operation is conducted.'10 Following fermentation, the weak alcoholic wash was transferred into a pot still for distillation. The still was usually mounted on a hearth of stones, heated by a peat fire. Heating the still drove the alcoholic vapours up into the head of the still and over into the 'lyne arm' which carried it down through the 'worm', a coiled copper pipe, submerged in a barrel or 'worm tub' filled with cold water which caused the alcoholic vapour to condense into a liquid known as 'low wines'.

A second, and occasionally third distillation provided whisky that was suitable for sale. Located at the base of the worm tub was the outlet or 'feedan' which allowed the spirit to flow into casks or other containers ready for immediate transportation. Illicit whisky was rarely matured for any considerable period of time as there was no economic incentive to let it age. The diagram in the plate section gives a representation of the type of still used by illicit distillers on Arran in the early 1800s.

A considerable number of illicit distillers on Arran were provided with distilling equipment by Robert Armour, a

Campbeltown coppersmith. The Armour family were prominent in illicit and legal whisky production in the Kintyre peninsula throughout this period. James Armour was found guilty of unlicensed distillation in South Argyll, c.1798. Other family members were connected with the formation of two legal distilleries in the town: Meadowburn in 1824 and Glenside in the 1830s. Robert Armour himself established a plumbing and coppersmithing shop in Longrow in 1811. This legitimate business was used as cover, concealing Armour's principle employment of manufacturing equipment for illicit distillers. Armour kept a detailed record of his transactions in account books, spanning the period from May 1811 to September 1817. These records were found amongst family papers and before their discovery very little was known about this aspect of unlicensed production in Scotland. Armour produced stills for customers throughout Kintyre, Gigha, and Arran. Over the six-year period, he manufactured approximately 400 stills, carrying out work amounting to the value of £2,000.[11] In relation to Arran, 53 transactions were carried out with island distillers who purchased equipment valued at £169 1s. 8½d.[12]

The stills produced by Armour were simple in their design, consisting of a body, head, lyne arm and worm. The complete apparatus could be purchased for less than £5 and consisted of approximately 30-40 pounds (lbs) of copper. In August 1814, Archibald Taylor and Thomas McCurdie of East Bennan, Arran, purchased a body, head and worm of 37lbs for £4 12s. 6d.[13] Dr IA Glen in her considerable analysis, *A Maker of Illicit Stills*, estimated that this amount of copper would have given Armour's stills a capacity of over ten gallons.[14] This correlates to McCulloch's first-hand account that illicit producers on Arran generally used stills of around 18 gallons capacity. Although professionally constructed, Armour's equipment was relatively inexpensive. New copper utensils were priced at 2s 6d per pound. Glen argued that the copper stills could have lasted for up to 20 years if maintained correctly. This being the case, purchasing an Armour still would have been a prudent investment for Arran distillers. Certainly, the accomplished, copper equipment manufactured by Armour would have provided them with a certain advantage over their illicit counterparts in other Highland regions, where cheap stills constructed from tin were used in many cases. While tin minimised the commercial losses in the event of equipment being seized by the gaugers, it drastically compromised the flavour of the whisky. It was recorded that, 'When spirits and acids came in contact with such surfaces, a portion of the metal is dissolved, and poisonous metallic salts are produced, which must be injurious to the drinker.'[15] The use of copper stills produced a vastly superior whisky, part of the reason why illicit Arran spirit was revered for its quality during this period. Undoubtedly Armours well-made and simple apparatus facilitated the production of vast quantities of high-quality 'peatreek'.

In addition to making new equipment, Armour also carried out repairs for Arran customers. In March 1814, he charged 13s for mending a still belonging to Neil Cook of Sliddery. James McKinnon sought his services for the repair of a still head in January 1815, for which he was charged 1s 6d.[16] The copper-smith sometimes re-sold used equipment, with William Currie of Corriecravie, purchasing an old still costing 12s in 1812.[17] Arran customers predominately paid in cash, but there was a limited degree of payment in kind. Occasionally old equipment and copper was traded in return for Armour's services. Commonly a lump sum of cash was given up front, with the final amount paid off in one or two instalments. Arran customers were typically prompt in clearing their debts, however it did take three years for Robert Black of Corriecravie to settle his account.

All of Armour's Arran customers were male, operating as individuals or as a pair. However, 20 per cent of his Kintyre clientele were female, and Arran women were known to play an important part in island distilling. It is likely that island men were charged with smuggling the stills across the sea from Kintyre, therefore Armour only had direct dealings with them. The transport of distilling equipment could be dangerous and costly. The unfortunate William Jameson of Torrylinn had a newly purchased body, head and worm seized from his possession by the Excise near Smerby, a settlement north of Campbeltown, on 24 August 1815.[18] Unperturbed by this loss, Jameson returned to Armour the very next day and purchased a near identical still.

Information contained in Armour's accounts confirms that the parish of Kilmory was a hub of illicit distilling and smuggling during the early 19th century. Armour's equipment was purchased by Arran tenants residing in 21 settlements located throughout the south and west of the island. The map in the plate section shows the approximate distribution of Armour stills on the island, emphasising the concentration of illicit distilling at the south-end. Sliddery residents were involved in 12 transactions, with the McKinnon family featuring heavily in dealings with Armour. Tenants at Western Bannen (Bennan) were involved in seven purchases. Various inhabitants of Corcravie (Corriecravie), Clachaig, Easter Bannen (Bennan), Torlinn (Torrylinn), Bennecargen (Bennecarrigan) and Shanachy (Shannochie), purchased equipment from Armour on three separate occasions. This included Daniel Cook of Bennecarrigan, the man accused of breaking an exciseman's leg in 1807, who admitted practising small-scale distilling during his trial. He purchased a 19-lb body and 11-lb worm in October 1815.[19] Evidently his previous altercation with the Excise had not discouraged him from partaking in unlicensed distilling.

The neighbouring Cooks of Margarich (Margareoch) were also heavily involved in illicit distilling. In November 1814, John Cook purchased equipment from Armour in Campbeltown. Six months later his son, John jnr, acquired a 13-lb worm for £1 12s 6d.[20] Another relative, Malkom Cook, purchased a still body in December 1811.[21] Armour's dealings with the Cook family demonstrate the cooperative nature of island whisky production. Like farming, distilling was carried out in a communal manner. It was customary for equipment to be shared between relations and neighbours so that they could distil from the barley they had grown on their own small piece of land. This was practised throughout Arran as John McCurdy of East Bennen was caught distilling with what he claimed was, 'a borrowed still' in 1808.

Armour's account books offer a key insight into the location of illicit still sites on Arran. They reveal common locational and geographical characteristics. Illicit distilling was carried out in isolated places, with a ready supply of fresh water. Mills and kilns were also located in close proximity, for processing grain prior to distillation. The settlement of Margareoch provided a perfect location for clandestine whisky-making. The clachan was near a remote glen, close to Sliddery Water, with its own corn kiln. Illicit bothies and huts, made of drystone walls and roofed with heather, were often constructed near settlements for distilling. It was documented in the 1850s that a dozen smuggling bothies and secret dens were discovered and destroyed by the Excise in the south-end. Arran residents also carried out distilling in sea caves. These natural coastal features provided a great deal of seclusion, in addition to allowing islanders to keep watch for approaching Revenue Cutters. McCulloch observed in 1819, 'the marks of fires, not improbably made by smuggling distillers,' at the sandstone caverns at Tormore, near Machrie.[22] It was reputed by John Henderson of Blackwaterfoot in the 1960s, that there was an old smuggler's cave on the shore between Imachar and Whitefarland. Henderson recalled:

> When I was young there was steps away down to it as broad as that. Now you have to crawl away down but when you go down on the flat,

the ceiling is higher than this yin. Oh, there was a willow tree hanging over the mouth o'it, you wouldn't know you were passing it unless you were told, and they had cut water from the burn to kill the smoke. They would need to be very smart gaugers if they ever caught them there.[23]

It was also common for stills to be set up in the open, protected by a bank or rock next to a burn. In the mid-19th century, Mr Evans of the Excise discovered, 'a temporary bothy, fixed over the rock', at Port-Bennan.[24] Open-air distilling reduced the risk of detection, as the location was not fixed. Therefore, at the first sign of the Excise, equipment could be readily hidden away. Not all distilling was carried out in bothies and remote regions. Widows and the elderly would have been less capable of making whisky in difficult locations. This class of islander distilled in outbuildings and their own homes. This made them vulnerable to detection, as Widow Wylie and aged John McCurdy found to their cost during the first decade of the 19th century (see pages 34-5).

The remnants of distilling bothies are dispersed throughout the remote Arran landscape to this day. Unfortunately, finding and identifying these sites is an extremely challenging undertaking for the simple reason that they were designed not to be discovered. Nonetheless, recent fieldwork aided by Forestry Commission worker Rab Logan's extensive knowledge of the Arran landscape has facilitated the discovery of the physical remains of an illicit whisky bothy on the island. The bothy lies in a coniferous plantation approximately 1km north-east of the abandoned settlement of Smuraig (NS 00792416). Located at the foot of a small hollow at the junction of two small burns, the structure is recessed into a crag, with three clearly defined dry-stone walls constructed in a rectangle shape, measuring approximately 4.5 by 2.5 metres. The south-west facing wall is the most complete, standing roughly 0.7m in height. The other walls are less intact and there has been considerable tumble within the structure. The photographs in the plate section clearly show the setting and structure of the bothy.

The characteristics of the 'Smuraig Sma' Still' are consistent with other illicit bothy sites that have been identified throughout Scotland, most notably at Badger Falls in Glen Affric and Platach Buide in Strathconon. Furthermore, when Rab Logan first encountered the site over 40 years ago he recalled finding fragments of copper, possibly from a pot-still or other distilling utensils. The physical make-up of the site, combined with its location, provides clear evidence that the structure facilitated illicit whisky production. The bothy is situated approximately two kilometres from the settlements of East Bennan and Levencorroch, known hot spots of unlicensed distilling in the early 19th century. As a clear example of physical evidence of illicit distilling practices on the island, the bothy has been put forward for inclusion in Historic Environment Scotland's database, which catalogues archaeological sites throughout the country.

Having undertaken their own archaeological survey of Arran using airborne laser scanning data in the summer of 2018, Historic Environment Scotland are particularly interested in locating still sites on the island. This is not the first time a detailed search for the remains of illicit distilling bothies has been made on the island. In 2014, using Geographical Information Systems (GIS) techniques, alongside field and soil analyses, Stirling University student and island native Hazel Ramage uncovered several potential small-still sites at Gargadale, an abandoned settlement to the east of the Ross Road (NR 957261). Ramage's initial research has been taken on by a number of students from Stirling University led by Dr Claire Wilson, who conducted further fieldwork examinations in the summer of 2017. The use of these innovative techniques has the potential to further unlock the secrets of Arran's distilling past. It is hoped that the insights offered by the recent surveys on the island will enable the identification of other whisky bothies, akin to the 'Smuraig Sma' Still', and provide further physical evidence of this illicit industry.

8

THE VOYAGE OF THE SMUGGLER

I T WAS RECORDED IN THE EARLY 1800s that Arran whisky could 'always command a sale.'[1] The substantial smuggling network, outlined in Chapter 3, facilitated the export and trade of illicit whisky. Not all smugglers actually made the whisky, and not all distillers were directly involved in the transport of their produce. Whisky smuggling, like many aspects of distilling, was a communal activity. Transportation was almost exclusively carried out by groups of young Arran men. Robert Brown noted that smuggling bands acted like *banditti*, escaping detection and excise officers at will. Arran smugglers developed a reputation throughout the west coast of Scotland, and were, 'respected for their intrepidity and daring.'[2] The parish minister of Kilmory remarked that:

> To the smuggler no stigma was attached on the account of his employment; on the contrary, it was considered rather an honourable occupation, as exhibiting an intrepidity and art that acquired for their possessor a distinction in the minds of his companions. It was in the darkest night, and in the most tempestuous weather, when no cruiser would stand the gale, that, in his little skiff, the smuggler transported his cargo to the opposite shores of Ayrshire.[3]

Clearly smuggling was a sought-after occupation, offering a degree of adventure and escape from the harsh realities of island life. Smugglers were revered throughout the parish for their almost open defiance of the hated gaugers. Whisky traffickers at the south-end of the island were deemed by Brown to be, 'much more ferocious than the other inhabitants of island.'[4]

Bands of smugglers would transport whisky from the bothies and clachans where it was distilled, to the small isolated harbours that dotted the Arran coastline, carrying it on their backs or by horse and cart. One of these inlets was known as Duncan's Port (NR 999208). According to the 1961 oral testimony of John Kerr, from Auchencairn, 'Duncan was a joiner in Craigdhu, and a smuggler as well, and this is where he shipped his illicit whisky, and the port is still in existence.'[5] It is likely that the aforementioned Duncan, was one Duncan Cook, a south-end tenant who was accused of attacking excise officers at Craigdhu in the 1850s (see Chapter 16).

At these small harbours islanders would load the whisky into small vessels, known as wherries. These basic craft were responsible for the safe transportation of smugglers and their precious cargo across the Firth of Clyde to the Ayrshire coast. The Arran wherry was described by novelist Robert Buchanan in 1871 as, 'a wretched-looking thing', that was, 'now nearly extinct.'[6] In July 1817, the wherry *Friends of Arran* was seized by the crew of the HMS *Driver* for conveying whisky without a permit. The vessel was listed as having; two masts, two gaffs, one bowsprit, one main boom, one mainsail, one foresail and jib, two rudders, one tiller, six oars and two anchors. Although primitive in their design, it was noted that these boats faced, 'weather before which any ordinary yachtsmen would quail.'[7]

Many wherries were in poor condition, due to the extreme weather they faced over the course of their smuggling service. In 1808, the wherry *Katty of Lochranza,* owned by John Kerr, was seized by a Revenue Cutter near Carradale Bay. Hidden in her cargo of potatoes was 40 gallons of illicit whisky. The condition of the seized boat was noted: 'she is extremely Leaky and by the salt water getting into her, so very much the Potatoes have become greatly damaged.'[8] It was a testament to the skill and

'Cottages at Corrie, Isle of Arran' by Henry Bright (1810-1873). This strong pencil drawing dates from one of Bright's Scottish trips in the 1850s and shows a typical example of an Arran blackhouse. *Courtesy of Guy Peppiatt Fine Art.*

The famous image of the MacAlisters' illicit still, taken in Donegal in 1902. The set-up with three men tending the still would not be too dissimilar from the same operation being carried out on Arran, but in a more secluded setting. *Chronicle/Alamy Stock Photo*

These accounts for Glenshant Distillery provide a unique insight into the workings of Arran's earliest licensed whisky-making venture between 1790-93.
Courtesy of the author.

A section of the 1799 Excise map of Scotland clearly illustrating the position of Arran within the Intermediate District between the Highland and Lowland Districts. *Courtesy of Scotch Whisky Archives.*

A 'sma' still' being worked in the Maramures district of north-western Romania where the practice of distilling fermented fruit is still widespread. *Courtesy of Ian MacIlwain.*

An illustration of an illicit pot still akin to the apparatus produced by Robert Armour, the Campbeltown coppersmith and still-maker, for Arran customers in the early 19th century. *Courtesy of the Forestry Commission.*

The crew of an unidentified Revenue Cutter cast a watchful eye over Lamlash Bay. Revenue vessels regularly patrolled the Firth of Clyde attempting to curtail widespread smuggling practices. The image probably dates from the late 19th century. *Courtesy of Stuart Gough.*

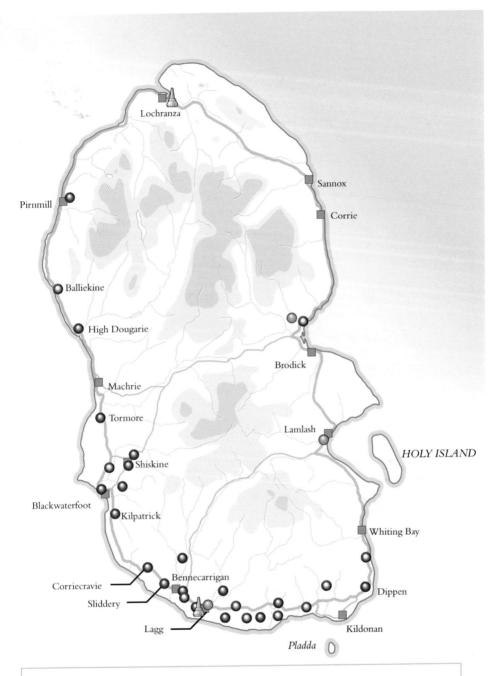

Lochranza

Sannox

Corrie

Pirnmill

Balliekine

High Dougarie

Brodick

Machrie

Tormore

Lamlash

HOLY ISLAND

Shiskine

Blackwaterfoot

Kilpatrick

Whiting Bay

Corriecravie

Bennecarrigan

Sliddery

Dippen

Lagg

Kildonan

Pladda

- 🔴 **Illicit still** site (*according to Robert Armour's Account Books*)
- 🔴 Site of a notable **whisky smuggling incident**
- ⚪ Location of a **legal distillery**
- ⚗ Location of **present-day distillery**

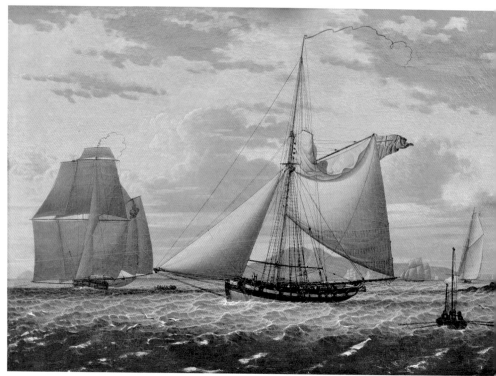

HMS Revenue Cutter *Wickham* by Robert W Salmon (1775–1851). Designed for both speed and seaworthiness the vessel was ideally suited to patrolling the west coast of Scotland and was commanded by an Arran native, Captain James Fullarton. In the background Arran and Ailsa Craig (far left) are clearly visible. *Courtesy of Argyll and Bute Council.*

The cottages, Shannochie, c.1900, the scene of the infamous killing of three Arran natives during a clash between islanders and the crew of the *Prince Edward* Revenue Cutter. Until the 1950s a memorial service was held near the site of the incident. *Courtesy of Stuart Gough.*

The headstone marking the final resting place of William and Donald McKinnon in Kilmory Kirkyard. Both men were fatally shot by a party of armed excisemen near Shannochie. *Courtesy of the author.*

The inscription reads:

SACRED
to the memory of
William McKinnon Tenant
in Torrilin who died 25th March
1817 aged 57 years and to that of
Donald his Son who died
the same day aged 22 years
they were both cut of by
a party of Sir John Reid
Cutter, headed by
John Jeffery Mate

Garden Street, Ayr, c.1920, the location of 'Auntie Bettie's smuggling agency' and frequented by Arran whisky traffickers in the early 1800s. *Courtesy of South Ayrshire Council Library.*

The Arran Clearances Memorial in Lamlash was erected in 1977 by the descendants of evicted families who were forced from their homes between 1829 and 1840. *Courtesy of the author.*

'The Whiskey Still at Lochgilphead' by David Wilkie (1785–1841) provides a fascinating insight into the workings of a small licensed Highland distillery. 'Old' Lagg distillery was also equipped with a spirit still of just over 60 gallons. *Courtesy of Bridgeman Images.*

nerve of the Arran smugglers that whisky made it to the mainland in these rudimentary, often unseaworthy craft.

The whisky transported in these wherries was stored in small casks or ankers, which held between eight and ten gallons (36-45 litres). It is likely that old rum, sherry, and brandy casks would have been re-used for this purpose. Local coopers would have also fashioned casks for smugglers and distillers. Arran residents were frequently caught transporting empty casks off the island's coast. In 1817, five empty casks were seized from Neil Currie. His plea of ignorance to this being a crime was dismissed, as his neighbour's boat had recently been apprehended for the same offence.[9] Whisky was also smuggled in smaller containers, including jars and flasks.

Negotiating the treacherous seas off Arran in modest vessels laden with whisky-filled casks was a challenging undertaking. Arranachs were renowned for their sailing ability, and it was asserted that, 'like all islanders, they are generally inclined to a seafaring life.'[10] Their skill and in-depth knowledge of local waters would have greatly aided their smuggling exploits, allowing them to outmanoeuvre the larger and faster Revenue Cutters that patrolled the Arran coast. To avoid detection smugglers often operated, 'amid darkness and tempest.'[11] Smuggling in these appalling conditions was highly dangerous and in some cases had fatal consequences. In December 1822, three Arran men lost their lives smuggling whisky to Ayrshire. The tragic incident was reported in the *Inverness Courier*:

> Malcolm and Angus Sellers, brothers, and Alexander Crawford, all natives of the Island of Arran, left Brodick, on Thursday last, the 27th in a small boat with twelve casks of smuggled whisky. It appears that the mast had been broken by the beam, and it is supposed, they were unable to keep the boat off the shore with the oars, and that when she had come into the broken water she had upset or filled with water, and the three named persons must have perished. Their bodies have not yet

been found. The boat and her materials, with four casks of whisky drifted on the beach between Saltcoats and Ardrossan, and were seized by one of the Custom house officers stationed at Saltcoats.[12]

The fate of the Sellers brothers and Crawford shows the risks facing whisky smugglers in their pursuit of profit. The weather and the sea were not the only threats facing Arran whisky traffickers. In the early 1800s, seven Revenue cruisers and cutters patrolled the seas of western Scotland. These vessels operated out of Campbeltown, and covered a vast coastal region, stretching from the Isle of Man to the Outer Hebrides. Their principle objective was to suppress the illegal trafficking of dutiable goods. After the defeat of Napoleon in 1815, these ships were commanded by highly skilled naval officers who tracked down smugglers with vigour and ferocity. The well-designed cutters were built for speed and were ideally suited for the perilous seas of the western coastline. Smuggling wherries were dwarfed by these government ships and illicit whisky traffickers could do little if they were approached by a speeding, heavily armed cruiser.

The *Wickham*, an Irish Revenue Cutter, was one of the vessels based at Campbeltown. She was commanded by an Arran native, Captain James Fullarton. According to Inglis, in his early life Fullarton served on a British man-of-war in France, under the command of Lord Wickham.[13] The commander was so impressed by young Fullarton's intelligence, superior manners, and handsome appearance, he suggested procuring him some form of advancement within the navy. Fullarton replied that he was not ambitious for promotion and merely sought the charge of one of His Majesty's cutters. This would allow him to, '... spend my time usefully and honourably in cruising the waters around my native island of Arran ...'.[14] His request was granted, and the *Wickham* was commissioned with Fullarton as her captain. Most of his crew were also Arran men. In 1814, five of the crew – Duncan

McDougal, Peter Nicol, Donald McAlister, John McKelvie and Donald McMillan – resided on the island.[15] It was recorded in the Old Statistical Account that some of the young men of Kilmory were employed, '... in the Revenue cutters, and Excise yachts.'[16] Islanders serving on revenue vessels negated some of the smugglers advantages, as they shared the same knowledge of local waters. It would seem however, that Fullarton and his Arran crew displayed a fair degree of leniency towards their fellow islanders. The captain defended the character of numerous island residents accused of smuggling exploits over the course of his career. In 1816 Fullarton retired from duty, his annual pension of £100 allowing him to comfortably see out his days on his beloved Arran.

Not all cutter crews were as compassionate in their approach to combatting whisky smuggling. Altercations between officers and smugglers became increasingly violent and bloody as the 19th century wore on. In 1819, Duncan Sillers, a fisherman from Imacher, was severely wounded in the arm by a cutlass blow, delivered by a member of the excise crew commanded by John Patterson.[17] The incident occurred after Sillers had fled the scene of a seizure carried out at Carradale, north of Campbeltown. The Arran native was in the process of purchasing 15 casks of illicit whisky from Kintyre distillers when the transaction was interrupted by a cutter crew. Sillers was caught, 'with a dram glass in his hands,' as it was customary for Highlanders to drink from the cask when measuring out illicit whisky during a sale. This incident not only records the life-threatening dangers facing whisky-runners, but also that there was a degree of interaction and co-operation between Kintyre distillers and Arran smugglers.

It is known from Robert Armour's records that Campbeltown distillers purchased equipment for their Arran counterparts during this period. In this incident, the distiller, Angus McMillan, conveyed the whisky from his home on the western shore of

Kintyre. Sillers purchased it for subsequent transportation to Arran and presumably onwards to the Lowland market.

Sillers was not the only Arran resident trading Kintyre whisky. Donald Robertson, a sailor from Blackwaterfoot, was accused in 1816 of being, 'a notorious smuggler.'[18] Robertson operated a small passenger packet between Blackwaterfoot and Campbeltown, receiving, 'a Salary for such a service from the Duke of Hamilton.'[19] He was however, running more than passengers across the Kilbrannan Sound. He was caught with three gallons of unlicensed whisky, with another six casks supposedly thrown overboard after warning shots were fired by excise officers as he sailed from Campbeltown harbour at midnight. His vessel the *Mary of Arran* was subsequently seized and his plea of ignorance dismissed as, 'a mere excuse as he must have sufficient experience, the more he had been detected and his property seized more than once before this time ...'.[20] From these incidents, it is clear than Arran smugglers were not dealing exclusively in locally distilled whisky.

Furthermore, it is apparent that legitimate vessels, including packets, and fishing boats acted as cover for smuggling exploits. An amusing article titled, 'Intrepid Smugglers' from the *Perthshire Courier* in 1822 provides a clear indication of this:

> On Tuesday forenoon, an Arran wherry, manned by three strong fellows, and to appearance laden wholly with potatoes, pushed into the harbour of Ayr with all the confidence of a fair trader courting inspection. This bold countenance, however did not prevent two custom-house officers who were on the spot from boarding the vessel; whether they had the benefit of previous information, or merely acted upon the notoriety of Arran smuggling, they immediately set about rummaging the cargo, and soon brought into view two casks of whisky. More might probably have been discovered had not the Highlandmen interrupted the process by cutting their cable and setting off to sea with their cargo, officers and all, in the sight of numbers on the beach, who were much amused with the spectacle. With the exception, however, of

having the glory and emolument of their capture turned into shame, the officers did not otherwise suffer, the smugglers having put them safely into the first boat they met with.[21]

Whisky was often concealed in innovative hiding places. In 1817, 4½ gallons of whisky contained in two jars was discovered onboard an Arran fishing vessel. The whisky jars were found, 'concealed in a Bag of chaff the other under a bed, and covered over with other articles.'[22] As a result, the boat was detained and the crew imprisoned in the Tolbooth of Campbeltown. The crew, consisting of, Daniel Kennedy, Alex McKelvie, Allan Bailie and Alex McMillan, all resided in Whiting Bay and stated their occupations as Fishermen and Cotters. In their petition to the Campbeltown Excise Court they asserted that the:

> Whisky which they had on board, for no intention of Smuggling, but as a necessary article for prosecuting the fishing as no Boat would come near them to sell their Herrings unless they were able to offer each man ... a dram of Whisky a practice which your Honours well know that prevails along the whole fishing Coast of the Country ...[23]

Whisky was an essential commodity for Arran fishermen, forming a key part of traditional trading customs in Highland regions. It was lamented by the master of the HMS *Driver*, Mr Anley, that this practice cost the Revenue approximately £1,200 each year.[24] In addition to exchanging whisky for fish, island fishermen undoubtedly sold and traded it in Lowland markets when they landed their catch. A concerned mother of one of Kennedy's crew wrote to Mr Anley, declaring, 'that she had given one of the jars to her son that he might dispose of it in the Low Country in order to furnish what he might want, as she had no money to give him ...'.[25] It was deduced from her correspondence that she had distilled the whisky herself. Her testimony rather undermined the crew's defence and proved that the whisky was in fact being smuggled to the mainland for sale, in order to raise cash for other commodities. Fortunately for Kennedy and his crew they were released without charge along with their vessel and allowed to return to Arran. The whisky however, remained in the custody of the Campbeltown Excise Office. This incident backs up the earlier assertion that women, the aged and the infirm, were predominately involved in production, whilst the menfolk, often employed at sea, ran the risk of smuggling the whisky to the mainland market.

Men working in the fishing industry played a key role in smuggling. It was stated in the early 1800s that Arran fishermen were at a disadvantage to their counterparts in neighbouring districts due to the, 'difficulty of getting the fish carried fresh to market.'[26] Smuggling would have eased the reliance on this variable source of income. Indeed, Kennedy's crew and Sillers of Imacher, supplemented this principle employment by dealing in illicit whisky. This contradicts Robert Brown's insistence that inhabitants of the north-end did not smuggle as, 'they are far more industrious in the fisheries.'[27] It appears that legitimate fishermen were involved in whisky smuggling; their seafaring knowledge enabling them to escape the full attention of the Excise and earn further income from their whisky smuggling. Approximately 90 fishing vessels operated out of the parish of Kilmory alone during this period. It would have been an unenviable task for the Revenue Cuttermen to detect which of these were involved in the shipment of illicit whisky.

Excise crews already had their hands full attempting to counteract the actions of groups of young Arranach professional smugglers. An incident from April 1819, gives an insight into the exploits of these smuggling bands. It was documented in Campbeltown Excise Letter Books, that the crew of the *Wellington* Revenue Cutter were charged with transporting a small 19-ton vessel, belonging to a Captain Dowie, from Ardrossan to Campbeltown. The party, consisting of five men and a boy, were commanded by deputy mariner, John Patterson. Their routine voyage was interrupted when, 'about six miles west of the Island of Pladda and about the same distance from the Coast of Arran, they observed two Boats receiving towards them in the direction of the Ayrshire Coast ... one Smack rigged the other Wherry rigged ...'.[28] Being suspicious of this activity Patterson took four of his crew in a small tender of Dowie's boat to investigate. Rowing close to the smack, named the *Revenge of Arran*, they discovered that it had a number of casks on board and four men. Patterson and his crew subsequently seized the *Revenge* and secured the smuggled whisky. Patterson then ...

> put two of his own Men on board of her along with the Smugglers and on sending her to the Tender he and three men remaining of his party proceeded in chase of the Wherry which made for the Arran shore and Gained about three miles on them while they were engaged with the Smack.[29]

After a lengthy pursuit during which they, 'saw the Wherry throw a Number of Casks overboard which floated by them', Patterson and his men caught up with the smugglers and executed another seizure. Aboard the wherry, *The Flora of Arran,* there were five men and only one remaining cask. The revenue crew proceeded to tow the *Flora* to the larger *Wellington,* picking up the jettisoned whisky casks on the way. On returning to the larger vessel there was a tense moment, 'From the great disparity between the Officers Party and the Smugglers ... particularly as some of them when lying alongside made an attempt to excite the rest to rescue the Seizure.'[30] The smugglers however, were restrained by one of their own, Finlay Cook. As a result, Patterson gave him the smack, 'in order to convey himself and the whole of the Smugglers ashore.'[31] After lodging the whisky and the wherry in the Excise warehouse at Campbeltown, Patterson, 'went back to Arran and got delivery of the Smack from Cook.'[32] In total,

Patterson and his crew confiscated 22 casks, containing 176½ gallons (802 litres) of illicit Arran whisky. It was well known that Finlay Cook was a notorious island smuggler; three years prior to this event, his wherry, *The Rose of Ayr*, had been seized by the excisemen.[33] Others in the smuggling party were identified as John Cook, John Stewart and Donald McKinnon.

When successful, smuggling was highly profitable. 'Arran Water' commanded the substantial price of 11s per gallon when sold in the Ayrshire market during the 1820s. It was reported that the island smuggler Duncan Sillers was, 'in possession of a few Hundred Pounds with which he dealt so extensively in the Smuggling of whisky.'[34] During his incarceration in Rothesay Jail however, he wrote to the parish minister of Kilbride, John Stewart, requesting financial assistance, claiming he had, 'not the wherewith to support himself in Jail, and besides he has a Wife and Family who look up to him for their subsistence ...'.[35]

The seizure off Pladda had been particularly costly for the group of Arran smugglers, losing them the potential income of approximately £80. Undoubtedly Patterson and his outnumbered cuttermen had won that round and Patterson in particular was singled out for praise, having demonstrated, 'zeal and activity on similar occasions.'[36] He was particularly adept at catching Arran smugglers, and had also led the party which seized 15 casks of whisky from the unfortunate Duncan Sillers in 1819 (see page 59). The following year he was rewarded for his endeavours, securing a promotion to the post of Boatman at Campbeltown.

Ayrshire was the main market for small-still Arran whisky during this period. Smuggling boats regularly ran illicit produce to remote areas of this vast coastline. In March 1817, 'a horse and cart with eight ankers Arran whisky containing about sixty gallons,' was seized near Irvine by Kilmarnock excise officers, assisted by a military party.[37] It was noted that smuggling into Irvine was, 'chiefly confined to whisky from Arran.'[38] The tragic drowning of the Sellers brothers and Alexander Crawford, outlined earlier in this chapter, reveals that whisky was also run into Ardrossan and Saltcoats.

Greenock was another popular destination for illicit Arran whisky. Smuggling into this port was a hazardous undertaking as the enclosed nature of the Firth of Clyde at this point increased the threat of detection. As a result, smuggled whisky was concealed on board legitimate trading vessels. In the 1840s, Member of Parliament Mr PM Stewart detailed this illicit trade in a speech to a Free Trade demonstration at Stirling:

> Some years ago I was shooting in Arran along with Lord Archibald Hamilton ... I required to set home on a day when no packet sailed, and the only conveyance was a large wherry, in which a farmer was taking wheat to Greenock. I entered his vessel, and discussed the corn laws over eighty bags of grain, and enlivened our discussion with a drop of Arran water which had never seen the excise.[39]

Additionally, whisky was landed on the coastline to the south of Greenock and transported over land to the town. In 1800, the Excise Officer Robert McGrigor was assaulted whilst attempting to carry out a seizure near Skelmorlie. It was alleged that John Kerr of Lochranza, Alexander Kerr, and Donald Kerr, both of Urin Beg, a settlement near the present-day Lochranza Hotel, were guilty of deforcing the officer. The Kerrs were accused of conveying five casks of whisky and three bags of malt, 'on the road leading in from Greenock.'[40] John Kerr was later detained and imprisoned in Rothesay Jail, with bail posted at £50. The fate of his accomplices was not recorded.

A small amount of illicit Arran whisky was also landed on Bute in the early 1800s. The Collector at Rothesay documented that there were a, 'few individuals occasionally buying for their own consumption a small quantity of whisky clandestinely brought to them.'[41] This whisky was landed by smugglers from

Arran, Kintyre and Islay in small boats, 'at any point of the coast; always at a distance from Rothesay.'[42]

The trade with Bute was small in comparison to the volume of whisky smuggled into Ayr at the height of illicit distilling. This port was the largest market for 'Arran Water' during this period. In the 1820s, this coastal town boasted 46 spirit dealers and 40 taverns. These drinking establishments served Ayr's booming population. The number of inhabitants in the town and its greater area significantly increased from 8,000 in 1801, to just under 15,000 in 1831. This rise coincided with a growing demand for small-still whisky among all drinking classes. A mere 15 miles of open water separated the south-end of Arran from this busy, flourishing port. Smugglers frequently made the crossing in their small wherries loaded with casks of high quality and much sought-after whisky.

James Paterson provided a detailed first-hand account of the dealings of Arran smugglers in the town in his documentary works, *Reminiscences of 'Auld Ayr'*, and *Autobiographical Reminiscences*, compiled in the 1860s and 70s. As a young man, Paterson worked as an apprentice printer at the *Ayr Courier* in the 1820s, lodging with an older woman who he referred to as 'Auntie Bettie'. She lived on Garden Street, which was considered an upper-class part of Newton. Paterson often mused how his landlady could afford such a comfortable lifestyle as, 'She had no viable means of existence save the interests of a hundred pounds ... and the trifles arising from her boarders.'[43] The reason soon became clear to him over the course of the summer and harvest months:

> We had a follow-lodger, himself a native of Arran, who occupied the same room with us. He was delighted at the prospect of the approaching midsummer fair, trusting to meet so many of his island friends and relatives. Happening to go home somewhat later one night, during the fair week, our surprise may be guessed when we found him, along with one or two other Arran men, busily employed in measuring off certain gallons of 'bead-twenty two' – the standard strength of Arran whisky –

into a sort of stock-cask, kept by 'Auntie Bettie'. The Highlanders looked a little suspicious of us, but being assured, in gaelic, of our innocence, they spoke very friendly, and offered us a dram. We drank their health and wished them success. 'Auntie Bettie' herself entered soon afterwards, and the process of supplying the stock cask was soon completed, when another dram round finished the proceedings. After placing the cask in its usual secure and secret place, temporarily depositing another seven gallon keg under our bed, the Arran men took their leave for the night. The cat was now out of the bag. We understood how 'Auntie Bettie' contrived to eke out her scanty means.[44]

Paterson further explained that, 'Smuggling was usually effected in this way: a wherry would run over with a load from Arran to somewhere on the Prestwick Sands, which was landed at night, and brought into "Auntie Bettie" on subsequent evenings. In this way she disposed of great quantities ...'.[45] Island smugglers were assisted by a number of supportive town residents, who also benefitted financially from their exploits. A significant number of Arran natives who were seasonally employed in this region also played a key role in the illegal whisky trade. The Arran factor, John Paterson stated that, 'The young men and women go in considerable numbers yearly to Ayrshire to service ...'.[46] These connections were critical to ensuring the successful distribution of island whisky.

In September 1811 a violent altercation between excise officials and Arran smugglers took place in the streets of Ayr. Alexander McKenzie, Alexander Kerr snr, Alexander Kerr jnr, James Nichol (alias Nicol), John Murphy, all of them residents of Kilbride clachan in the parish of Kilmory, and Archibald Cook of Shannochie were tried at the Ayr Circuit Court, accused of assaulting and deforcing officers of the Revenue. It was alleged that the Clerk to the Excise Collector had received information that a quantity of smuggled whisky had been landed on the 'Coast of Ayr' and was to be brought into the town on the night of 23 March 1811. The Customs House clerk, assisted by James

Campbell and John Taylor, both tidewaiters at the Port of Ayr, proceeded along the public road from the town to the new Bridge of Doon in search of the smuggled articles. As they traversed the road, about a mile south of Ayr, near to a row of houses called Gateside and another settlement by the name of Bridgehouse, they happened upon a band of smugglers transporting three casks of smuggled whisky.

As they attempted to secure the casks the officers were violently overpowered by a large group of islanders. It was reported that James Campbell, 'was so much stunned as to be driven down on his knees and had a pistol which he held in self defence wrested out of his hand and carried off ...'.[47] His fellow tidewaiter John Taylor fared little better as he 'was struck to the ground ... kicked on his sides and limbs till he was rendered insensible, and was so much injured that he was thereafter with difficulty removed to a house in the neighbourhood and was from thence carried to Ayr where for a considerable time after he was confined in great pain and danger ...'.[48]

The islanders quickly fled the scene and disposed of their valuable contraband. Over the next few days a search was made for the culprits of the outrage and on 29 March, Alexander Kerr jnr, James Nicol, John Murphy and Archibald Cook were apprehended and brought before John Murdoch, the Sheriff Substitute of Ayr. Alexander McKenzie and Alexander Kerr snr were able to successfully evade the authorities with McKenzie making a daring escape by, 'leaping from the Window of a house during the period which a search was [made] to apprehend him.'[49] It was established that Archibald Cook and John Murphy had sought refuge with Cook's sister, Helen, at her lodgings in Wallacetown, whilst Alexander Kerr jnr and James Nicol were sheltered by John Black, a grocer from Newton. Black's harbouring of island smugglers suggests that Arran contraband was retailed through his grocery shop.

Understandably, the accused were unwilling to admit that the distribution of smuggled whisky was the reason they were lodging in the town. All claimed that they had departed Arran in a small fishing vessel with the sole purpose of purchasing seed corn. Their stay in Ayr was to last considerably longer than intended as the four Arranachs were incarcerated in the Tolbooth of Ayr until their trial on 6 September 1811. Alexander Kerr snr was to join them during proceedings, having finally been apprehended by the authorities. Alexander McKenzie was never tried however, as he had passed away before the case was heard in court. It is not known whether or not his window-leaping exertions contributed to his demise.

It was reported that the trial lasted most of the day with the jury not returning a verdict until the early hours the following morning. After hearing all the evidence, the court was informed that, 'it is abundantly clear, that the panels had been engaged in the smuggle, and that three of them had been guilty of the assault and deforcement.'[50] The jury returned a guilty verdict against Alexander Kerr jnr, Archibald Cook and James Nicol, and of 'not proven' in the case of Alexander Kerr snr and John Murphy, who were dismissed from court. The three guilty Arran men were sentenced to a further six months imprisonment, and seven years banishment from Scotland.

Unperturbed by the considerable risks and harsh penalties, Arran natives and residents of the Ayrshire coast continued to rebel against the Excise. It was reputed that local farmers along the coast were heavily involved in smuggling activities, harbouring islanders and their precious cargo. Paterson remarked that three cartloads of Arran whisky was seized by the Excise on a farm near Prestwick in the 1820s. Assisting smugglers was a dangerous occupation, as one farmer by the name Dow found to his cost in 1824. He was involved in landing Arran whisky on the sands between Monkton and Troon at the dead of night. During proceedings, the party was disturbed by a group of local seamen, who had been drinking in nearby Troon. One of the men, by the name of Johnstone, threatened to inform the Excise of the goings-on unless he was paid in money and whisky. His offer was refused and a scuffle broke out, during which Dow was fatally stabbed in the groin by Johnstone.[51]

This was not the only deadly calamity directly resulting from Arran whisky smuggling. In 1805, the *Chester Chronicle* reported the following incident in Ayr:

> Late on Friday night last, two men from Arran, carrying some kegs of smuggled whisky up the path leading from the Ducat stream to the Mill Vennal, having let one of them fall, by which the cask was so injured that the whisky was running out, applied to a gentlewoman for some vessel in which to put it, that the spirits might not be lost: she shewed them into a back-house, where, placing it in a washing tub, they went in quest of one of their country women, who has long been in the habit of assisting this illicit trade, with whom they soon returned, accompanied by a respectable old woman, who lived in the neighbour-hood, and began to run it off into another vessel, the gentlewoman of the house holding a candle, a spark from which falling into the spirits, it went off with an explosion, that drove the roof from the house, set the womens' clothes all in a blaze, and before any assistance could be afforded them, they were burnt in so shocking a manner, that the old woman expired the next morning, and the recovery of the other two remains very doubtful. The two mercenary smugglers, who had been the guilty cause of this cruel calamity, regardless of the alarming situa-tion in which they saw the three unfortunate sufferers, and callous to their piercing cries, deliberately snatched up two kegs of whisky and ran off, and hid them in a neighbouring yard. The honest indignation of the people, however, directed the search of two Excise Officers, who seized them. We much lament that the punishment the law allows of impressing [press-ganging] smugglers was not put in force on these unfeeling miscreants, who might easily have prevented the accident from proving fatal.[52]

It must be noted that many of the traditional tales of illicit distilling portray the smugglers as 'noble Highlanders' forced to defend their liberty against the brutal oppression of the hated Excise establishment. In reality, driven by a combination of greed and desperation, a number of whisky smugglers acted in a shockingly callous manner with little regard for human life. Unfortunately, many innocent bystanders were caught up in their fight against the excisemen. Nonetheless, many mainland farmers, townsfolk, and exiled Arran natives were inclined to assist island smugglers due to the widespread disdain for the imposed system of taxation and the potential financial rewards. The reality was that from the still mouth to the point of sale, a vast and sophisticated smuggling network was in place. This enabled smugglers to circumvent the Excise and distribute considerable quantities of 'Arran Water' into the Lowland market.

9

ILLICIT WHISKY CONSUMPTION

D ESPITE THE RISKS AND FATALITIES, smuggling and distilling continued to flourish in the early 19th century. William MacKenzie argued that on Arran, 'the taste for spirits encouraged the making of whisky.'[1] There is certainly some truth in his statement. Whisky formed a key part of Highland culture and traditions, and had become hugely popular in the growing urban centres of the Lowlands. In towns such as Ayr, illicit Arran whisky commanded the price of 11s per gallon which was considerably higher than the legal alternative.[2] Unlicensed spirits were sold and consumed in a fairly open manner in numerous taverns, groceries, and spirits dealers. It was well known that Andrew McCulloch, who kept a tea shop in Ayr, made a comfortable living trading drink brought over from Arran that was a lot stronger than tea.[3]

The quality and reputation of Arran whisky resulted in it being enjoyed by the elite of society whose traditional social lubricants of brandy and claret declined in popularity due to disrupted trade during the Napoleonic War, and a degree of patriotic opposition to the consumption of French spirits. As a result, high-quality native whisky gradually became the accepted tipple amongst the upper classes. Paterson suggested that 'Auntie Bettie', his bootlegging Ayr landlady, 'was well known amongst the more respectable class of people ... and few were above the temptation of purchasing "bead twenty-two" of Arran water.'[4] It was widely rumoured in the town that the Sheriff Court officials and the gentry of

Wellington Square regularly enjoyed a dram or two of smuggled Arran whisky. Undoubtedly there was a degree of truth in this gossip, as it was frequently documented that the upper classes were renowned for their enjoyment of illicit spirits. Arran factor Robert Brown lamented, 'I am afraid that illicitly distilled whisky finds its way to the tables of many gentlemen in the north.'[5] Furthermore, it was understood that the gentlemen of Ayrshire, 'never asked nor answered' where they procured their malt whisky.[6]

Indeed, on Arran, some of the more respectable members of society were directly involved in illicit smuggling and consumption. In 1816, Dr John Stoddart of Strabane personally arranged the shipment of smuggled whisky to Hamilton as part of a University Bursary gift.[7] In 1825, the innkeeper at Lagg, John McKinnon, paid his rent in whisky directly to the Arran factor, amounting to £11 6s 6d.[8] The tenth Duke of Hamilton personally enjoyed a dram or two of Highland spirits. In 1845 he instructed his factor, John Paterson to procure three gallons of whisky, priced at 15s a gallon, from James Bannatine (Bannatyne), innkeeper at Lamlash. Earlier, in 1836, it was documented in the *Evening Chronicle* that the duke, 'entertained a portion of the inhabitants of Brodick Bay to a dance in Mr Jamieson's Inn.'[9] It was observed that he attended in 'full Highland costume', and the festivities were, 'kept up with great spirit till seven in the morning.'[10] The tenth duke clearly enjoyed himself when he visited the island.

In was reported in the 1850s that when undertaking his yearly fishing expedition to Loch Earsie (Iorsa), the 11th duke would invite 30 or 40 of his tenantry to accompany him for, 'feasting and drinking on the side of the loch.'[11] These events were always well supplied with casks of whisky. In 1881, a 'Sale of the Cellar of Extraordinary Rare and Choice Old Wines of a Nobleman', was advertised in the *Glasgow Herald*. Listed in the inventory of the auction was a selection of, 'very Old and Fine Glenlivet and

Arran Whisky.'[12] Intriguingly, this notice reveals that some illicit island whisky was matured for a significant period of time, although in a rather unintentional manner. Certainly, the cellared spirit must have tasted quite extraordinary.

Arran whisky was popular at both ends of the social scale. Whisky that was not exported to the mainland was enjoyed by many islanders during social gatherings and festivities. It was documented in the national newspaper, *The Newcastle Journal* in 1840, that, 'At a wedding lately celebrated at Shedog, Arran, the whisky drunk amounted to the moderate quantity of seventeen gallons.'[13] This is equivalent to 110 modern bottles – there must have been a number of sore heads the following morning. At an earlier wedding at Dippin in 1805, a number of guests were reprimanded by the Kilmory Kirk Session for, 'drinking spirits to the degree of intoxication ... and that the Bridegroom exceeded as much as any of them.'[14] These gatherings were vital to forging a sense of community on the island, giving residents the opportunity to come together in celebration.

In the 1840s, the growing number of drinking establishments on the island was lamented by both parish ministers. There were nine public-houses at this time; three at Lamlash, two at Brodick, and one at each of the settlements of Lagg, Shedog, Lochranza, and Corrie. Angus McMillan, the Kilmory minister, voiced his dismay at the growing popularity of these establishments, suggesting that, 'their influence is pernicious, which is still the more grievous as their existence is unnecessary. More individuals addicted to spirts are to be found in their vicinity, than anywhere else in the parish ...'.[15] Kilbride minister, Allan McNaughton, was less scathing in his description of these inns, complementing them for being, 'very neat and clean, and occupied by families of respectable character and conduct.'[16] He deplored however the, 'small whisky shops in different parts of the parish, which contrive dangerously to elude the scrutiny of the excise; and afford the lovers of ardent spirits the opportunities of indulging their favourite beverage, without the public notice which they would incur by frequent visits to the licensed public-house.'[17] These small dramshops were full of illicit Arran stock, and facilitated the local consumption of unregulated whisky. Nonetheless, there were rarely reports of over-indulgence and the wider issues of violence and destitution associated with heavy drinking culture. Rural areas like Arran, for the most part, did not experience the same drink-related social problems that blighted the crowded Lowland industrial towns and cities as the popularity of ardent spirits increased throughout the 19th century. The production, rather than consumption, of spirits on Arran was a greater hindrance to law enforcers and excise officials.

Whisky consumption was an important aspect of Arran life, playing a key role in social gatherings and festivities. The drinking of Arran 'peatreek' also played a key role in the regional fishing industry, as demonstrated by the antics of Kennedy and his Whiting Bay crew (see pages 61-2). Furthermore, whisky and kelp gathering were heavily interlinked in the early 1800s. The kelp industry formed a key part of the communal Arran economy during this period. Kelp was used in the manufacture of glass and soap providing seasonal employment and additional cash revenue. In the early 20th century historian William MacKenzie interviewed an old Arran native, born in 1816, who recalled that whisky was an essential commodity during the kelp harvest along the exposed south-end. It was a cold and wet business, but the whisky provided much needed sustenance. This is a keen insight into the relationship between islanders and their whisky – it was an essential part of their everyday lives.

In the early decades of the 19th century a dram of whisky undoubtedly became a daily necessity for many islanders as their traditional way of life came under increasing scrutiny from the forces of agricultural improvement.

10

THE AGE OF IMPROVEMENT

IN THE WINTER OF 1828-29 upwards of 1,500 people, approximately 20% of the island population, were cleared from their Arran homes.[1] This mass displacement was the culmination of a process of 'modernising' the islands communal system of agriculture. As outlined in Chapter 2, for centuries Arran farming was carried out following a run-rig system based around small clachan settlements. During the late 18th and early 19th centuries this traditional agricultural system came under intense scrutiny throughout Highland regions of Scotland. Increasing population, urbanisation, and commercialisation of the market in the Lowlands created a significant demand for agricultural produce and key Highland goods, including cattle, kelp, whisky and wool. The Highland agrarian economy was viewed as archaic, inhibiting Scotland's development by failing to meet this growing market demand. As a result, various 'improvements' were advocated and implemented by agricultural reformers in an attempt to commercialise the Highland economy and destroy the traditional Gaelic way of life.

Arran in particular was viewed as 'backward' economically by advocates of agricultural development. MacCulloch described the island economy as 'antiquated', even though it was, 'situated at the very door of commerce and civilization.'[2] Many social commentators of the early 19th century believed that Arran's considerable economic potential had gone untapped. This was attributed to the attitude of the Hamilton dynasty, who were regularly lambasted for the lack of development on the island. The trustees of the seventh duke did however, sanction a degree of reforming strategies in the late 18th century. In the years following agricultural reform on the Hamilton family's considerable Lanarkshire estate in the 1760s, provisions were made for the re-organisation of Arran's agricultural system. The young duke's agent, John Burrel, was the man tasked with implementing an improvement scheme on the island. Burrel boasted that after his reforms there would not be a, 'single inch of community left in the whole island.'[3]

His intentions were clear; the larger communal farms were to be divided into two or three smaller holdings, controlled by a single tenant. Rigs and common ground should be enclosed and sub-letting would be forbidden. It was common practice on Arran, and many other Highland regions, for a section of agricultural land to be divided off for the children of a tenant. This was then run as a separate unit, with the offspring acting as subtenants. Furthermore, under the traditional system there were small plots of land, or single houses or cottages, occupied by cottars who paid rent in kind and labour rather than paying money. In 1810, it was documented that there was a significant number of this cottar class who were heavily involved in illicit whisky-making.

If these customary practices were prohibited, one tenant became responsible for an entire, formerly communal, clachan with the sole responsibility of making rent. Ultimately, Burrel's plans ended in failure. His insistence that high rents equalled high agricultural yields placed too much pressure on new single tenants and he was deeply unpopular throughout the island. It was lamented that his original plan caused tenants to, 'run into great arrears, of no less than Three Years rent, and of necessity [they] soon became bankrupt ... '.[4] The new single occupancies were simply too expensive for one family to run successfully. Burrel's initial impact was limited and it is widely agreed that his main accomplishment was the erection of head dykes between each farm in order to prevent the straying of cattle. By 1807 however, one island visitor stated that these barriers were useless. Subsequently, his plans were abandoned and the practice of communal farming continued on a significant scale into the 19th century.

Nonetheless, Burrel's legacy on Arran slowly eroded the island's traditional agricultural system. His principle of competitive tenancies destroyed the concept of security of tenure which was vital to local farming communities. Under Burrel's scheme, the sitting tenant of the new single farms risked being outbid and dislodged at the end of his tenancy. This system obliterated the centuries-old tradition of the same family retaining a lease and holding a clachan together for several generations. Arran tenants were now faced with a no-win situation; if they were unable to make rent, which larger farmholders were unable to do as a result of rent increases implemented by Burrel, they were evicted. Burrel's ideologies certainly had a negative impact on island tenants, starting the protractive process that would see many of them removed from their native land in the 1820s.

In 1810, William Aiton, when reporting to the Board of Agriculture, condemned the failure of the ninth Duke of Hamilton's improvement schemes on Arran, declaring, '... it is the fault of the proprietor alone that those in Arran have not become as intelligent, industrious, and liberal as the people in their rank on the other side of the firth.'[5] Aiton also noted that he observed the widespread continuation of communal farming during his tour of the island:

> [I] was truly sorry to see such a valuable island as that of Arran, and so much capable of improvement, remaining, in the nineteenth century, under the same barbarous system of management that it had been under for two centuries back ... the occupiers of land living in townships of four or five or twenty or thirty families ... sometimes a single ridge is subdivided into twenty lots occupied alternatively by as many people.[6]

In 1814-15, the second stage of agricultural improvement began on the island. It could be strongly argued that the public condemnation of the duke provided the key stimulus. Finally, Burrel's basic plan was implemented on Arran. The duke's chamberlain, Robert Brown, was instrumental in the re-organisation of the landholding system. Larger farms of 100 to 400 acres were marked out for mainland farmers from the Lowland counties of Ayrshire, Renfrewshire and Lanarkshire as, 'no local man had the capital or experience to handle units of such size.'[7] In 1816 the farm of Bennecarrigan was:

> ... lately taken by a tenant from Ardrossan, who, enticed by the comparative lowness of rent, fancies he is going here to make his fortune all at once ... To make room for this Improver, there has been an entire clachan or township of 16 or 20 native tenants removed: But these, I believe, have not left the island, but are set down in smaller possessions, one by one ...'.[8]

The remaining, old communal farming units, rather than being consolidated, were divided into smaller lots which were leased to single families.

Up until 1815, the number of farm units on the Hamilton's Arran estate was 113. Each one had between four and 12 sub-tenants, usually relatives of the main tenant. During the 1814-15 re-organisation, these sub-tenants were given their own separate holdings, between two and 40 acres, raising the number of farms to 458. Fifty-three of these were significantly larger units. The policy of enclosure was recorded by a contributor to the *Farmer's Magazine* who observed that the townships of the south-end, 'have hitherto been occupied in common, or in the run-rig system, yet now they are to be laid off in severalty as the leases expire; each tenant having his own part distinct from the rest.'[9] Tenants were monitored carefully. Hedges were planted to separate the new smaller units and strict regulations laid down regarding crop rotation and the rearing of livestock. Sheep were prohibited except on stock farms, and goats were forbidden as they were deemed, 'troublesome and unprofitable.'[10] This agricultural reform was focused on the southern half of the island, with arable farming concentrated on the coastal regions of the south-west.

Undoubtedly these changes had a profound impact on the island inhabitants. MacKenzie noted that the changes, 'could not be carried through without effecting a revolution in the economic system and so in the social habits and outlook of the people.'[11] He further commented that the reforms decimated the communal nature of the agrarian economy to the detriment of the island community: 'Every tenant was now on his own. He was an individual in the eye of the estate, not a member or representative of a group. He could be dealt with in isolation; the combination of the hamlet community had been dissipated.'[12] Writing 80 years later, Little confirmed this observation, arguing that by 1815, 'most of the clansmen of the southern part of the island had probably resigned themselves to the destruction of their traditional communities.'[13]

11

THE CRISIS OF 1815-17

THIS PERIOD OF INTENSE agricultural reform coincided with a shift in landowner attitudes regarding the practice of illicit distillation and smuggling. During the first decade of the 19th century, agents of the duke displayed a degree of leniency in their dealings with known distillers and whisky smugglers as it was widely accepted that these illicit activities ensured regular rent payments. In 1812 however, there was a significant grain shortage on Arran as the island harvest was greatly damaged by a prolonged period of poor weather. Consequently, requests from Arran tenants for relief and rent abatements markedly increased. This was met with great displeasure from the factor, Robert Brown, who attributed the islander's plight to their own illicit activities:'... I confess my feelings are not readily moved by complaints from people who choose to make part of their grain into Whisky and then cry want in order to raise the pity of the proprietor ... '.[1] Therefore Brown had,'... no intention of giving any Meal to the Inhabitants ... knowing that they could supply themselves better than I could.'[2] The following year with much of Scotland facing near famine conditions, legal distilling was prohibited to ease the pressure on grain supplies. Illicit production further increased to meet the demand for whisky, worsening the plight of renowned smuggling regions, such as Arran.

Illicit distilling and smuggling on the island was becoming increasingly troublesome and, perhaps more importantly, unprofitable for the island's main landowner. It was documented by Brown that in 1814:

> When I began to introduce a complete change of the letting of the island, and to lot the farms, and to make roads under the commissioners of the Highland roads and bridges, erecting new farm-houses, and bringing in Low-country tenants, some of the people who inhabited the district where smuggling prevailed, and in communication with the Irish, carried off the road-tools, and began to break down some of the new houses we were building; and on investigation, I understood it was those smugglers who had got lawless in their intercourse with the Irish, and likewise with smuggling into the low country, that were guilty of the outrage ...[3]

Clearly, smuggling and illicit distilling were providing a barrier to the improvement schemes advocated by Brown. There was a sense of disorder and lawlessness on the island with tenants carrying out offences against the estate and the Revenue almost at will. Following his tour of the island in 1819, John MacCulloch lamented that:

> The pernicious practice of illicit distillation and of consequent smuggling, to which the situation offers strong temptations, has greatly contributed to the depravity of the people, who, in losing some of the characteristic virtues of the Highlanders, appear to have acquired in return, only the vices of that civilization to which they have so free access.[4]

Brown heavily criticised the local excisemen for the escalating situation on Arran. He claimed that their actions allowed distilling practices to get to, 'a considerable height.'[5] The system by which the local excise officials operated was blamed for the high degree of illegal whisky production. Brown recorded that when fines were levied they were not collected immediately, suggesting that officers, 'were not over anxious to entirely destroy a system ... from which they derived a considerable revenue.'[6]

In 1815, the Excise levied significant fines against Arran illicit distillers, however their collection was not enforced until 1817. During the first half of that year another £700 worth of fines had been racked up by unlicensed distillers. It was estimated that upwards of £4,000 in excise penalties remained outstanding on the island at this time.[7] As a result, the proceeds of unlicensed distilling went towards clearing this debt, rather than the payment of rent. The re-organisation of agricultural units and rent increases in 1814-15 had already placed the small tenant distillers under considerable economic strain.

As rent arrears increased, tensions between Brown and the excisemen escalated. He felt strongly that their actions were a major contributing factor to the desperate situation on the island. His contemporary Alexander Young noted that, 'the soil of the Island, instead of being cultivated for the benefit of the of the Proprietor and the people, or even for the use and advantage of the State, is in fact a sort of Common for the Harpies of the Revenue.'[8] Young stated that the profitability of the duke's holding was being undermined in order to, 'fill the pockets of the officers of the Revenue.'[9] He added that it was Brown's duty to, 'protect the poor people from Fiscal oppression.'[10]

As a result, the factor adopted his own prohibitive measures by instructing his ground officers, Dr Stoddart and James Davidson, to undertake a search of the island in order to seize and destroy illicit stills. It would appear that they were particularly dedicated to this task. In a letter to Brown, Davidson wrote that, 'We have been pretty successful in discovering Stills, about fifteen have been found out without going to the South end, we are going to that District today where there is every reason to expect a greater number.'[11] In 1822, Brown recounted details of the search for illicit stills: 'I sent out the people I had under me managing the island, and we seized to a very great number in one day, I think nearly thirty.'[12]

Furthermore, Brown implemented a scheme whereby he attempted to procure a considerable proportion of the island barley by giving tenants credit on their rents. The acquired grain was then sold in the markets of Greenock and Glasgow, 'in place of distilling it into whisky.'[13] The success of this arrangement was limited as considerably less grain was willingly handed over than expected. Furthermore, in the face of dwindling resources of local bere and barley, islanders began importing this key ingredient from neighbouring Kintyre. Davidson wrote that Arran illicit producers were, 'so much set on distillation that they are purchasing ground Malt from Campbeltown in large quantities, indeed it is said that the importation is greater this year than was known before …'.[14] The procurement of processed barley directly from Campbeltown maltsters would have negated the issues of supply and saved Arran distillers the troublesome and time-consuming task of converting barley themselves. Additionally, Dr Stoddart noted that, 'Very little bear has been recovered from the South … I am informed they are carrying it to Ayr …'.[15] Davidson revealed that it was being conveyed to the mainland in liquid form, stating that, '… the Tenants pretend that they can send it easier to Air than to Brodick, but the truth is they are determined to continue in their old favourite practice of Smuggling.'[16]

The local excise authorities were apparently outraged by Brown's interference in revenue matters. Arran officer Mr Munn was accused of, 'endeavouring to persuade the people to retain their Stills telling them I [Dr Stoddart] had no authority to demand them …'.[17] The excisemen were clearly in no mood to surrender their main source of income. Officers were paid a modest salary and heavily relied on the proceeds of their seizures. By destroying a still, the opportunity of accumulating financial gains from further fines was lost. The majority of their earnings were derived from the judicial sale of the produce of a confiscated still after a fine had been levied on the perpetrator at the excise court.

The Arran excise responded to Brown's actions by collecting outstanding fines and enforcing harsher penalties on those caught distilling without licence. Those who could not pay in cash were threatened with having their cattle seized. It was even claimed that officers stated that they would sell off islanders bedclothes in order to raise what they were owed.[18] It was documented in January 1817, that the Excise showed 'no mercy' in their actions with, 'two parties ransacking the Country for a week ... '.[19]

The Rothesay Supervisor, Mr Forrester, arrived to oversee proceedings, it being suggested that, 'his intentions are very unfavourable, they are levying the old fines in the first place very quietly but making the poor people pay very high expenses no less than ten shillings for every pound of fine.'[20] Forrester was said to be, 'much dissatisfied with the destruction of the Stills ... [informing] the people that they were fools and that they all be recorded for prosecution.'[21] Davidson wrote to Brown declaring that, 'I am much afraid that a number of small tenants will be ruined by the high fines discerned against them ... '.[22] He claimed that, 'there will be nothing left to pay the rents with by the smugglers ... '.[23]

In response to the heavy-handed approach of the Excise and the apparent crisis on the island, solicitor Alexander Young met with the Board of Excise in February 1817 on Brown's behalf. Young expressed concerns regarding the actions of local officers, the levying of high fines, and the delay in their collection. The Chairman of the Board, Woodbine Parish, admitted that, 'the fines which had been imposed upon the people were excessive and ruinous, and were so intentionally, as inducing the only means to check the illicit trade.'[24] Young mused that the board's chief objective was, 'to urge on us the establishment of a legal distillery under the authority of the late act, the apparatus for 40 gallons being no expense ... '.[25] Parish had only recently been appointed Chairman of the Excise and he was immediately faced with numerous challenges. The output of legal distilleries was dwindling and consequently so was the cash paid in duty. This forced him to examine ways in which the revenue could be augmented by encouraging legal distilling, particularly in Highland areas, and eradicating endemic illicit production. To achieve this, Parish reduced duty rates and introduced the 1816 Small Stills Act. This legislation allowed the use of stills throughout Scotland of no less than 40 gallons, permitted the use of weaker washes, and finally abolished the disastrous Highland Line. It was therefore little surprise that Parish was actively encouraging the formation of a legal still on the island. Brown however, was unimpressed with the Board's response:

> I have no objection whatever to the fines being high for the greater they are the better, but I wish the board to be aware of our very important circumstance and that is their fines are never immediately uplifted on being inflicted but the parties fined are indulged until such time as they can pay by means of the profits arising from additional frauds against the Revenue ... Instead therefore of acting as a preventative the fines in the way they are collected have served as an additional indictment to the continuation and extension of the practices complained of indeed it consists with my own knowledge that none are so active in smuggling as those who have a fine hanging over their head of which they are anxious to be discharged.[26]

Brown demanded that the excisemen on Arran be dismissed and replaced by 'proper officers,' stating that:

> ... if they continue the same set of Officers and allow them to consider themselves as permanent Settlers in the island and earning a steady income from the frauds of the smugglers the fines will be collected slowly out of the profits of the illegal trade and the present practices will remain undiminished.[27]

He concluded by stating that when the Board implemented this measure he would be, 'ready to bring forward proper people to begin work from the 40 Gallon stills according to the suggestions of the Board.'[28] As a result the Board came to the resolution of, 'dismissing the whole of the Officers now employed in Arran, and to replace them with an entire new set ... '.[29] The unfortunate officials, Mr Munn and Mr Forsyth, were re-posted to Beith and Stranraer respectively, whilst the Supervisor, Mr Forrester was sent to Castle Douglas.[30] Young wrote to Brown expressing regret that, 'they were not sent a greater distance from the Island than the opposite coast of Galloway, from whence they may probably be able to Keep up a correspondence with their quondam friends in Arran.'[31] Brown however appeared pleased with the outcome, ominously stating that now, 'the Board with our assistance can easily crush the practices complained of ... '.[32]

Resident island distillers were caught in the crossfire as agents of the Duke of Hamilton and the excise authorities sought to curtail illicit activities without damaging their own financial wellbeing. The seizing of stills and imposition of heavy fines greatly compromised their already perilous financial position. Islanders were already under pressure from alterations to the traditional agricultural system and subsequent rent rises. As a result, Arran tenants were becoming increasingly desperate in their struggle to maintain their traditional distilling practices. When stills were seized in 1817, they, 'were given up with much resistance ... '.[33]

This confiscation of equipment was lauded as a success by Brown and his contemporaries. It was noted by the Excise however, that when this measure had previously been implemented by local officers, 'the inhabitants had practiced a deception on them, he believed in many instances by producing old implements and keeping up the newer ones, and that he feared that the destruction was not so effectual as could be wished, there being some more of the stills, still in activity.'[34] This was certainly the case in 1817 as illegal whisky distilling continued to be widely practised after Brown's initial search. Davidson wrote to Brown in the months after the still seizures outlining that:

> ... it will require the strongest measures possible to make them give up their favourite employment (smuggling) which will ultimately tend to their ruin if permitted to be continued. Although the Messengers and Excisemen are going through the Island everyday, I am told they are as throng as ever making whisky.[35]

By this stage it was recorded that many of the small tenants were experiencing considerable financial hardship. The pressure was building on illicit distillers and many islanders were becoming increasingly distressed as they were squeezed financially by both the Excise and the actions of their own landlord. In March 1817, Davidson warned that the islanders were, 'more resolute than ever,' in carrying on illicit distilling.[36] Whisky-making, a vital part of their culture and economy, was coming under increasing threat. Islanders had already witnessed the virtual destruction of their communal agriculture and were unwilling to surrender another key element of their island existence without a fight. Tensions between locals and their oppressors escalated, reaching breaking point on 25 March 1817, when smugglers and excise officers clashed in one of the most infamous incidents in Arran's history.

12

THE WHISKY KILLINGS, 25 MARCH 1817

O N THE AFTERNOON OF this fateful day, William McKinnon and his son Donald, set sail from the south-end with a cargo of smuggled whisky. After proceeding a short way they noticed the *Prince Edward* Revenue Cutter which had been observing them. They immediately put about, heading for the safety of the Arran shore but the mate of the cutter, John Jeffery, was ordered by his commanding officer Captain Sir John Reid to lead a party to investigate and seize any smuggled articles. Jeffery and his 12 heavily armed sailors landed on the shore near the farm of Shannochie (Shanochy).

They proceeded to search the surrounding area and discovered four casks of illicit whisky which had recently been, 'landed from a boat, and taken up the country to Shanochy moor.'[1] It was documented that the seizure took place approximately four miles from the shoreline. In the course of returning the casks to their vessel, Jeffery's party was joined by four or five islanders who, 'declared themselves the perpetrators of this breach of law.'[2] William McKinnon was one of them, apparently offering to help carry the whisky to the shore, in return for a dram. McKinnon declared that he could be trusted as he had been in the service of the Revenue for 13 years. His offer was refused and as the crew continued towards the shore, the smugglers were joined by a curious group of islanders who, 'followed close upon Mr Jeffery and his party ...'.[3] As the size of this gathering increased, Jeffery ordered his men to fire two blank warning shots to disperse the crowd. This action was ineffective, serving only to raise the hostility and animosity of the gathered islanders. Tempers started to flare as heated words were exchanged between the crowd and the excisemen. It was alleged that the islanders threatened the officers declaring that, 'none of the crew should return to the cutter with their lives.'[4] Breaking point was reached about half-a-mile from the shore near the 'Shanochy houses' when the assembled party rushed forward violently in a desperate attempt to reclaim the seized whisky. As a result Jeffery, a hardened naval veteran, ordered his men to open fire on the crowd. The excise party, armed with muskets, pistols and cutlasses, unloaded a total of nine rounds at the unarmed islanders. This heavy-handed response was deadly, killing both McKinnons and a local woman, Isobel Nicol. William McKinnon was shot through the body, uttering the cry, 'Good God, Donald, I am gone,' as he fell to the ground.[5] He lingered until the evening, when he finally succumbed to his injuries. His son, Donald was shot through the breast, and died within a quarter of an hour despite the desperate attempts of the local minister, Mr Crawford, to dress his wounds. Isobel Nicol died about an hour and a half after the clash, suffering two fatal musket shots to her body. During the fracas a young boy, Peter Crawford was also badly wounded after being shot in the knee. Following the violent confrontation the crowd quickly fled, allowing the crew to return to their vessel with the four casks of whisky, leaving the dying and wounded where they fell.

This bloody altercation was met with uproar on Arran. Davidson warned that following the incident, islanders were, 'showing strong symptoms of Rebellion ... '.[6] Subsequently, Jeffery was tried for murder at the High Court in Edinburgh. The trial took place on 9 September 1817, gathering widespread publicity with court proceedings reported in numerous national newspapers including: *The Scotsman, Caledonian Mercury*, and *The London Courier and Gazette*. This interest was understandable due to the potentially scandalous nature of the case. Jeffery was a distinguished officer, acting on behalf of the British state, under the direct command of an eminent figure in Scottish commerce, Sir John Reid, who was a partner in the mercantile house of Reid, Irving & Co, established c.1790 by his father Sir Thomas Reid. At the time of the trial Sir Thomas was a director of the East India Company, where he also served as chairman on two separate occasions in 1816 and 1821.

Sir John himself would go onto surpass his father's achievements becoming a director of the Bank of England in 1820, a post he held for 27 years, ultimately serving as governor from 1839-41. He also represented the Tory party as the Member of Parliament for Dover from 1830-1 and 1832-47. If Jeffery was found guilty of murder, it was conceivable that the spotlight would have shifted on to Reid and his role in the incident. This implication would have considerably damaged his personal reputation and interests, blackening the name of a prominent and influential Scottish family.

Reid was not the only member of society's upper echelons who would have been concerned by the case brought against Jeffery. Agents of the Hamilton estate, having only recently demanded, and then implemented, tougher measures against island smugglers, were now faced with the 'murder' of three of the duke's tenants. The successful conviction of Jeffery would have severely undermined their drive to eradicate the illicit island economy. Compounding matters was the fact that Jeffery conducted his actions under the authority of the British state. With the economy faltering following the end of the Napoleonic Wars in 1815, there was widespread unemployment and high food prices, fuelling social unrest. This led to renewed calls for increased democracy through reform of the parliamentary system. Furthermore, throughout the Highlands there was increasing discontent and turmoil as the ruling elite introduced new land-use policies, which forced people from their homes. In response to this, there were occasional outbreaks of violence, most notably during the Kildonan riots of 1813, when tenants of the Marquis of Stafford forcibly protested against their removal to make way for sheep farming. In this period of increasing social tension, the conviction of an agent of the government for the murder of unarmed civilians would have damaged the authority of the established order. If Jeffery was convicted of this capital offence, there would have been considerable implications for some of the most influential members of Scottish society, undermining the actions of the landed elite and the British state.

In this uncertain social and political climate, the islanders search for justice, or even the right to a fair trial, was to prove futile. From the outset, their case against Jeffery was hindered by a number of factors. Firstly, the presiding trial judge was the Lord Justice Clerk, Lord Boyle. During his time as a serving Member of Parliament between 1807-11, Boyle was a vocal supporter of the prohibition of all forms of grain distillation, both legal and illicit.[7] He was therefore in no way inclined to be sympathetic to any persons engaging in an activity he had publicly deplored. Lord Boyle was not the only participant in court proceedings who was unmoved by the fate of the unfortunate islanders. The Edinburgh jury, drawn from the capital's privileged society, were men who habitually regarded Highlanders with a degree of contempt, sharing the popular view that as 'Celts' they were racially inferior to Lowland Scots who were of 'Anglo-Saxon' heritage. These were men akin to the Edinburgh-born John Pinkerton who categorised Highlanders as, 'indolent, slavish, strangers to industry.'[8] Arran natives at this time were described as, 'although honest in their dealings with one another, they frequently, like the Jews, think it no great crime to get as much as they can from strangers, or those in a situation above them in rank.'[9] When the jurors heard the Gaelic testimony of island witnesses, delivered through an interpreter, they were unlikely to have any empathy with a people divided from them by not only language, but a deep-rooted and racist ideology.

From the outset it was highly unlikely that the islanders expectation of justice would be delivered. In fact, it was a testament to their determination and sense of outrage at the killings that Jeffery was charged with murder and the case even made it to the High Court. Certainly, legal precedent was firmly on the side of Jeffery and his actions. Despite frequent clashes throughout Highland regions between gaugers and smugglers, only a handful of cases involving the fatal injuring of whisky traffickers by excise officials were brought before the High Court in the late 18th and early 19th century.

These cases included the trial of Patrick Anderson in 1799, who despite killing an Aberdeenshire smuggler by administering multiple cutlass blows to his back, was found 'not guilty' of culpable homicide.[10] In 1813, the case of Hugh Chalmers and others was brought before the High Court. It was established that an excise party, led by Chalmers, had ambushed a group of smugglers coming into Glasgow from the Highlands, down the Garscube Road. During the ensuing scuffle, two of the smugglers were shot and killed. Again, the excisemen were dismissed without charge.[11] It was remarked by the renowned Scottish advocate and historian, Sir Archibald Alison, that, 'Most of the trials, of late years, for homicide by [Excise] officers of the law, have terminated in the same [not guilty] result.'[12]

The islander's legal counsel would have had to present a compelling case to ensure the conviction of Jeffery. This however, was not forthcoming. Acting on the islanders behalf was Solicitor-General James Wedderburn (Counsel for the Crown), Samuel McCormick, and JA Maconochie. The prosecution delivered an eloquent indictment, declaring that Jeffery, 'conceived a causeless malice and ill will against the said persons, [and] did feloniously and barbarously himself fire a pistol loaded with ball at the persons so assembled.'[13] Despite this strong opening statement, the case against Jeffery quickly faltered in the face of an intense legal challenge from his defence team. He was represented by the renowned Edinburgh lawyers, George Cranstoun, Francis Jeffery, Alexander Wood and John Hope. Interestingly, both George Cranstoun and Francis Jeffery had been employed by the Hamilton estate to settle a number of prior legal disputes. Less than two months before John Jeffery's case was heard, Cranstoun had successfully represented the estate's interest in a land dispute with Miss Ann Douglas Hamilton (latterly Westenra) the illegitimate daughter of the eighth duke. Cranstoun also developed a personal relationship with the tenth duke, dining with him at Hamilton Palace. Francis Jeffery had been involved in proceedings when the ninth duke mounted legal action against Mrs Scott Waring in 1815.

Both Cranstoun and Jeffery, having obtained satisfactory outcomes during previous legal proceedings, had secured the trust and favour of Robert Brown, saving the estate and the ninth duke himself, from considerable financial cost and embarrassment. In a similar regard the conviction of John Jeffery had the potential to damage the interests of the estate, undermining the strategic suppression of the illicit Arran economy in order to help push through agricultural reforms. Certainly, if Jeffery was convicted (and sentenced to death) the newly appointed excise officers on the island would have been less enthusiastic about ruthlessly suppressing smuggling activities for fear of potential legal reprisals.

Robert Brown and his legal contact in Edinburgh, Alexander Young, having campaigned and petitioned the Excise for over a year in order to facilitate their strategy for suppressing all illicit activities, were in no mood for anything to undermine their efforts. Unsurprisingly, both were enthusiastically supportive of

Jeffery's actions, with Young declaring that, 'I am glad to see in the Newspapers that the Arran Engagement has been with the crew of the Revenue Cutter, it will give a proper lesson to the Inhabitants which I hope will be followed up by great vigilance and attention on the part of the new Excise Officers.'[14] Evidently, agents of the Hamilton estate had little regard for the welfare of their island tenants, and were more concerned with ensuring that excise officials could be relied upon to implement the strategy of 'annihilating illicit distillation in the Island of Arran.'[15] In this climate, it is not hard to imagine Brown and Young manoeuvring and using their legal connections to secure Jeffery trusted legal representation in the form of George Cranstoun and Francis Jeffery, and ensure that the correct, 'not guilty' outcome was brought in.

There is no firm documentary proof to confirm that the Hamilton estate machine was directly involved in securing legal counsel for Jeffery. What is certain however, is that John Jeffery, an excise official on a modest salary, was able to call upon two of the most shrewd legal minds of the day. Francis Jeffery, in partic-ular, was renowned as an effective advocate who was able to bend a jury to his will. It was asserted that over the course of his career Jeffery had, 'won a more questionable reputation by obtaining acquittals of some reputed criminals.'[16] In 1812, he infamously defended Helen Kennedy of Dumfriesshire who was tried for fatally poisoning her neighbour and his servant with arsenic-laced porridge. Despite clear evidence of her guilt Kennedy was saved from the gallows by Jeffery's legal skill, which apparently bewildered the jury. It was recorded that at the trial Jeffery's examination of key witnesses was, 'extreme ... he made them seem to say almost what he would, and blocked them up from saying what they evidently wished to say.'[17] During the trial of his namesake Francis Jeffery would adopt a similar tactic, using his legal and verbal prowess to undermine the evidence of Arran witnesses during cross-examination. Islanders called to the stand were coaxed into implicating themselves in assisting with transporting and concealing the smuggled whisky. Daniel MacKinnon, the first Arran native called admitted that, 'he saw the smugglers bring up the whisky, and he helped hide it.'[18] James Cook, another key witness for the crown prosecution revealed that he, 'went to the shore, to try [to see] if he could save any of the whisky.'[19] This was a sound legal strategy, completely discrediting the testimony of the islanders, and presenting the witness and the victims as the actual subverters of established law and order.

This tactic built on the defence's opening statement which emphasised Jeffery's naval service.

> Mr Jeffery, the panel at the bar, entered early in life into the navy, at the age of eleven; and from 1803 till 1814, when he entered into the service of the Customs, he was employed in various situations in the course of his profession, and displayed the coolness and intrepidity, characteristic of the profession of the British navy ... he had been, in the course of his profession, in upwards of 30 battles against the enemies of his country ... having spent the greater part of his life in exposing it by combats with the enemies of his country, I trust he will not be obliged to lay down, under sentence of the law, a life which he has often fearlessly exposed for his country's benefit.[20]

At a time when the Napoleonic Wars were still fresh in consciousness of the British public it was an astute tactic to present Jeffery as a distinguished naval veteran, who, when conducting his honourable duty, was violently confronted by a lawless 'mob' who had no regard for the authority of an officer of the crown.

As the trial continued, a widely diverging series of events was presented by islanders and members of the excise crew who were called as witnesses. Mariners Peter Jenkins and Alexander McQueen claimed that a crowd of 200 people converged on the excise party. It was stated that the islanders acted in an aggressive manner, throwing a number of stones which twice struck the sailor James McCulloch on the back as he carried a cask of whisky. Island witnesses disputed these claims, declaring that the crowd was around 40 or 50 in number, mostly made up of women and children. Jenkins further alleged that Jeffery had frequently told the assembled crowd to 'keep off', but they insisted on harassing the party. Apparently, when the two warning shots were fired the islanders gave a 'hurra' and rushed over the fence at Shannochy in order to attack the excise crew and reclaim the smuggled whisky. Having been knocked to the ground, Jeffery commanded his men to open fire in a desperate attempt to disperse the crowd.

Arran witnesses maintained that there had been, 'no violence offered to the party; or any stone thrown.'[21] It was however, decreed by both sets of witnesses that the crew fired after Isobel Nicol and another woman, Isobel Shaw, attempted to seize a cask from one of the sailors. This sparked the ensuing rush and prompted Jeffery to give the order to open fire on the crowd. When pressed as to why Isobel Nicol acted in such a manner, local tailor Daniel Kerr informed the court, 'that she was a rash clever woman, and had no idea of the danger she run.'[22] He supposed that she fully intended to reclaim the seized whisky.

From the surviving newspaper reports and court records, the events of this fateful day remain unclear, due in part to the contradictory evidence offered by both sets of witnesses. By the conclusion of the trial however, the testimony of the Arran natives had been emphatically discredited. Undoubtedly, the skilful defence mounted by Cranstoun and Jeffery, aided by the lack of conviction and preparation on behalf of the prosecution, contributed to the acquittal of John Jeffery. In a highly unusual incident, the Solicitor-General effectively conceded the case during his closing statement, admonishing all guilt from Jeffery, and blaming the actions of the islanders for the fatal outcome of the incident:

The only reason which induced me to detain the Court so long by the evidence which has been adduced, was, that from that part of the testimony which consisted of that of the islanders (as it may be characteristically called), I did entertain some doubt and hesitation as to the charge of murder, for, from the beginning, I was satisfied that this charge was inapplicable to the case – but whether, if these witnesses had spoken truth, there was not room to think the homicide was in some degree rash and culpable. This part of the evidence, however, has been more favourable to the panel than even in the precognition; and the evidence of the men belonging to the cutter appeared so fair, that all my doubts have been removed. The result of the inquiry has been clearly to show, that the character of an useful officer in the public service stands unimpeached, and that he has done his duty with a manliness and [sic] which reflect on him the greatest credit. And, in the next place, the result of the investigation has been, or, I trust, in your opinion will be – to show those lawless persons, who trust to impunity from their remoteness from the seats of justice, this is impossible, with safety to themselves, to assault or endanger the lives of public officers ... In a word, I submit, that the Jury are bound to return a verdict in every respect favourable to the panel.[23]

Understandably, counsel for John Jeffery was firmly in agreement with this assessment, with Francis Jeffery declaring:

Undoubtedly, it is very rare that so cordial an agreement should prevail upon the two sides of the bar. Unfortunately, it is rare that any proceedings of this most painful and distressing nature should terminate in a way so completely agreeable to all sound principles and liberal feelings. Even after the evidence which was brought on the part of the Crown ... has been in favour of our client ... As far as the forms of Court permit, therefore, I say, we are certain of his receiving an honourable discharge; and we shall not endeavour, by any evidence as to his general deportment, or as to the particulars of the transaction in this unhappy affair, to show that the sufferers were not chiefly, but solely to blame. In these circumstances, I trust I do not fail in my duty to my client, in trusting entirely to an honourable acquittal ...[24]

In conclusion, the presiding Lord Justice Clerk, Lord Boyle, informed the jury:

> I have no difficulty in stating to you, from the evidence disclosed, not only by the persons belonging to the revenue vessel, but from that drawn, some part of it with reluctance, from persons who took a considerable concern in the transaction, there is no ground for a verdict in terms of this indictment. Throughout this unfortunate day, the conduct of the pannel [Jeffery] was most distinguished for moderation, propriety, and determination to so the duty incumbent upon him by the office he held under Government, for his country. Therefore, I have no doubt it is your duty, and will give you satisfaction, to find he is not guilty of the charge in the indictment.[25]

The jury returned a unanimous verdict of 'not guilty' without leaving the courtroom. In his closing remarks, Lord Boyle assured Jeffery that, 'while you conduct yourself, as you appear to have hitherto always done, according to the same rules of humanity, propriety, and proper public spirit, there will be little probability of a similar charge ever preferred against you in any criminal court.'[26] In the end, the Arranachs' protestations that Jeffery and his men had murdered their neighbours and relatives had been disregarded as the officer walked free from court. Given the social and political unrest of the time, the outcome of the trial was never in doubt. The conviction of Jeffery would have fuelled discontent and dissidence, fortifying local resistance to infringements and actions which threatened the illicit economy of Arran. A combination of the skewed legal system and the influence of the powerful Hamilton estate ensured that this outcome was avoided, and Jeffery's violent response to smuggling activities was vindicated.

The events of 1815–17 marked a dramatic shift in attitudes towards the illicit island economy. Smuggling was publicly deplored, with men of standing like Robert Brown and Alexander Young affirming their commitment to eradicating the, 'great moral and political evil of smuggling.'[27] The benefits of supporting Arran's black economy for the island elite were now outweighed by the negatives. Distilling no longer ensured financial gain for the Hamilton estate via regular rent payments, serving only to fuel social unrest and violence against agents of the established order. Whisky smuggling was increasingly viewed as a barrier to the agricultural advancements advocated by the improvers, including Robert Brown. Evidently, his campaign to curtail illicit distilling at this time formed part of his larger improvement plan for the island. The successful implementation of this strategy was dependent on the removal of apparently corrupt excise officials and the assurance that newly appointed officers would be able to assert their authority without fear of reprisal and retribution.

Subsequently, islanders were caught in a perilous situation as the Excise, supported by the agents of the Duke of Hamilton, sought to suppress, rather than encourage illicit distilling and smuggling. The tragic events of 25 March 1817 reveal the increasing desperation of the islanders after one of their key activities was placed under significant threat. As they were squeezed financially, they were forced to resort to extreme measures in a frantic effort to retain a few gallons of whisky. The willingness of a large number of residents to aid the McKinnons by taking on heavily armed officers, without thought for their own safety, demonstrates the communal element of smuggling. Whisky production formed a critical part of the island way of life and was worth fighting for.

This sense of defiance survived on the island in the years immediately following the events of 1817, with Arranachs continuing to violently resist excise officials. In 1818, Shannochie tenants James McBride and Peter McKenzie, alongside James Nicol, a tailor residing at Lackievore (Leacamor), were accused of smuggling whisky into Ayr. Having been caught in the act, the three Arran men allegedly attacked local officers of the Revenue.[28] Curiously, given the increasingly authoritarian approach to suppressing clandestine whisky activities, none of the men were convicted. James McBride's case was dismissed, as it was apparent that he was not directly involved in the smuggling and merely in the wrong place at the wrong time. Both McKenzie and Nicol successfully evaded justice and despite being outlawed they were never brought before a court to answer for their supposed crimes.

These isolated acts of rebellion were to prove futile as Brown's vision for the eradication of Arran's illicit whisky economy was significantly aided by the introduction of radical new Excise legislation in the early 1820s. These developments combined to irreversibly alter the economy and social conditions of the island into the latter half of the 19th century.

13

EXCISE LEGISLATION
IN THE 1820s

I N 1820 THE FOURTH DUKE OF GORDON, one of the largest landowners in Scotland, made a speech in the House of Lords highlighting the problem of illicit distillation in the Highlands. He advocated legislative changes that would encourage legal distilling practice in the north of Scotland and ensure that landowners would do more to actively put down illicit distilling and smuggling. In light of this declaration, the Fifth Commission of Inquiry into the Revenue was set up to investigate the distilling industry in Scotland and Ireland, under the chairmanship of Lord Wallace.

In 1822, before the commissioners report was published, the inquiry led to the passing of the Illicit Distillation (Scotland) Act. This legislation significantly raised the penalties associated with carrying out illicit distilling and smuggling. Justices of the Peace (JP) were instructed to enforce minimum fines of £20 or a six-month jail sentence for persons convicted of the practices. Those caught using unlicensed stills could be fined up to £100, whilst smugglers convicted of transporting illicit spirits faced penalties of £200. The discretionary power of the JP to reduce fines in cases of hardship was removed. Furthermore excisemen were given additional authority, including the power to remove or destroy equipment without a warrant from the JP. They also received a monetary reward for each detection. This amendment to excise legislation ensured that there was now a financial incentive for officers on Arran to effectively destroy stills, a measure that Robert Brown had strongly advocated since 1816. As the Excise received greater landowner support and financial motivation to suppress the illicit distilling industry, the number of detections increased significantly throughout Scotland. In 1822 alone, 4,867 persons were convicted of unlicensed whisky production.[1]

The 1823 Excise Act, based on the findings of the Wallace Commission, supplemented this tough policy towards illicit distillation and smuggling. This key Act reduced the duty on legal spirits by half (to 2s 5d a gallon of spirits produced) and introduced a universal licence fee of £10 for the right to distil. This government intervention made it viable to conduct small-scale legal distilling in Scotland for the first time. As a result, between October 1823 and October 1824, 134 new licensed units were set up throughout the country.[2] In the Highlands, the number of legal distilleries increased from 46 in 1823 to 101 in 1828.[3]

The effect of the two Acts was dramatic. By 1832, the number of persons detected distilling without a licence had fallen to 144.[4] Finally, it appeared that lawmakers had settled on a formula that maximised revenue from spirit duties and discouraged illicit distilling and whisky smuggling.

On Arran the introduction of this new legislation reaffirmed Brown's plans regarding the eradication of unlicensed production. In 1822, the Collector at Rothesay wrote to the Board of Excise remarking that on Arran, following the passing of the Illicit Distillation Act, 'practices highly injurious to the public revenue and to the people themselves have very considerably diminished and will we trust soon be put an end to.'[5] Initially, however, not all local magistrates were willing to levy the new high fines, undermining the new legislation. John Thomson and John Ballantine of Issa Water, Buteshire, were fined the modest sum of £10 in 1823, after being convicted of smuggling 11 gallons of whisky across the Kilbrannan Sound.[6] In other Highland regions, JP continued to be lenient on convicted distillers. At a JP Court in Inverness in 1823, over 400 persons were charged with crimes against the Revenue. All received a fine of less than 20 shillings.[7] This attempt to undermine the new policy was counteracted by the excise establishment, which transferred some local cases to the Court of Exchequer in Edinburgh. Here, Arran smugglers felt the full force of the inflated fining measures. In 1823, Neil McKelvie of Auchencairn, near Whiting Bay, was fined £200 for bribing and obstructing an excise officer at Ayr.[8] In the same year, Gavin Hamilton of Arran was fined £40 for obstructing officers at Ardrossan. The fine was subsequently raised to £200 after he failed to appear in court.[9]

Nonetheless, some islanders remained determined to carry on illegal whisky production. In 1826, the *Glasgow Herald* reported that an Arran family consisting of a father, son, and daughter, were incarcerated and fined £60 after they were found guilty of illicit distilling at the Rothesay Excise court. Although the family, 'bore the appearance of great destitution,' they were released from jail within a week after paying the considerable fine.[10] It would appear that illicit distilling was still a lucrative business, or the episode may have revealed the communal nature of the practice on Arran. In the Outer Hebrides it was noted that people frequently joined together to pay off large fines enacted by the Excise. The liberation of the destitute family might indicate that this practice was also common on Arran as it is doubtful they would have had the means to pay off the large fine by themselves in such a short time.

The report in the *Herald* further noted that, 'These cases show that the practice of illicit distilling is far from being cut up by the new laws, and that something ought still to be done to do away so mischievous an abuse ...'.[11] Despite misgivings in the press, excise officials continued to praise the effectiveness of the new legislation. Officer John Harvey stated in 1824 that:

We have reason to believe that it has been considerably decreased, that it is not carried on to the same extent in Argyle, and that in Arran, Dumbarton and Greenock, and places round. In many places where illicit distillation was carried on to our knowledge, it has been greatly abolished, and there has been a great demand for legal spirits.[12]

Officials like Harvey had reason to be confident in the new Excise system. High fines were not the only measure inhibiting illicit production; the lowering of licensing and duty rates increased legal production significantly. This was further aided by the introduction of malt 'drawback'. Legal distillers were now able to reclaim 1s 2d per gallon of whisky produced solely from malted barley. These actions effectively acted as a reduction in tax, negating illicit distillers production and cost advantages by encouraging legal producers to use larger quantities of malted barley. As a result, the quality of licensed Highland whisky improved dramatically. Subsequently, a number of renowned illegal producers took out licences in the 1820s, most famously George Smith of Glenlivet. Major landowners were now actively encouraging legal distilling in an attempt to enhance the income from their estates. This was certainly the case on Arran, as the Duke of Hamilton and his agents advocated the establishment of a legal still on the island following the alterations to the excise laws (see Chapter 15). The new legislation was certainly effective, with the volume of duty-paid whisky doubling from 1823 to 1824, reaching over six million gallons (27m litres).[13] By the early 1830s, it was documented by excise officers and estate factors that illicit distilling was a thing of the past in the traditional heartlands of Islay, Kintyre, and Perthshire.[14]

Arran, however, remained troublesome with unlicensed practices lingering into the 1830s. It was recorded in 1834 that on Arran, 'illicit distillation had been and still is practiced to an extent seldom equalled in the neighbouring islands. The smugglers give a better price for the grain that is thus used, than the tenants can obtain in any other way, and hence a demoralizing and, in the issue, a profitless tendency and traffic is kept up.'[15] It was further stated that from, 'the prevalence of this unlawful employment, the natives have acquired a reserved and suspicious manner ...'.[16] It could be argued that the island's isolation due to continuing transport difficulties contributed to the persistence of the illicit trade.

By the late 1830s however, illegal distillation and smuggling activities had been checked significantly. In 1840, the Kilmory minister Angus McMillan recorded that, 'Illicit distillation prevailed til a very recent period, to a very considerable extent, but within the last ten years, very decided measures were taken for its suppression, and it is now almost entirely done away.'[17] Kilbride minister, Allan McNaughton, attributed this reduction to, 'the heavy fines imposed of late on convicted delinquents and the diminution of the gains of smuggling by the improvement of the spirits manufactured by the licensed distiller ...'.[18] Arran factor, John Paterson confirmed the demise of the illegal trade, declaring in 1837 that, 'Illicit distillation, which prevailed to a great extent, has now nearly altogether ceased.'[19]

14

THE CHANGING NATURE OF ARRAN

THE VIRTUAL ERADICATION OF illicit distillation and smuggling dramatically altered the cultural and economic make-up of the island. The illegal industry had been vital to the early 19th-century Arran economy providing vital cash income and additional employment for some of the poorest members of society. This helped to facilitate a period of sustained population increase on Arran; the number of inhabitants rose from 5,179 in 1801, to 6,541 by 1821.[1]

As illicit whisky production and trade declined throughout the 1820s, the island economy faltered. Rent arrears increased dramatically as islanders struggled to find a legitimate market for their grain. This problem was exacerbated by falling prices of cattle and wool, the other staples of the island's agricultural economy. Furthermore, there were limited alternative employment opportunities on the island outside of farming. By 1822, the kelp industry had virtually collapsed as Scottish producers were undercut by the lowering of import duties on Spanish barilla. Whereas island whisky was much sought after with a great reputation, Arran kelp was thought to be of inferior quality to the produce of other regions of the Western Highlands.[2] In reality, the industry was not particularly profitable to the duke's estate or his island tenants. Therefore, when many Arranachs were forced to give up illicit distillation and smuggling, they had no alternative means of income outside the meagre returns from their small agricultural holdings.

Arran was becoming a considerable drain on the Hamilton estate, with arrears amounting to over £3,000 in 1820.[3] Clearly, harsher penalties and increased vigilance from the local excisemen had impacted islanders' capability to make rent, particularly in southern regions. It was noted by Brown in the early 1820s that tenants in the north of the island, '... pay better rents, and pay more punctually than in the part where the smuggling is carried on.'[4] In 1822, the newly appointed Arran factor, John Paterson, submitted his annual report to the duke, confirming that the island economy had become a serious concern. By the late 1820s, the tenth duke and his agents were becoming increasingly impatient with the lack of progress on the Arran estate. Drastic action was required that would allow them to fully implement their improvement schemes and stimulate the faltering local economy. As was the case in so many areas of the Highlands, mass eviction and forced emigration was deemed to be the most practical and profitable solution. Paterson argued that the island was becoming increasingly over-populated:

> As the people marry young, and little emigration has hitherto taken place from the island, the whole population now may safely assumed to be nearly seven thousand, a population by far too great to be subsisted on the island, with little profitable employment and few means of subsistence farther than are furnished by the soil and a herring fishery, and this fishery has for the last nine years been almost a complete failure.[5]

Paterson dismissed the promotion of economic diversification to ease the pressure on agriculture and provide legitimate alternatives to employment in unlicensed distilling and smuggling. He argued that, 'the forced introduction of manufacturers among the population and their progress, even if introduced, would be very tardy.'[6] In any case, Paterson claimed that this would involve a considerable financial risk given, 'the present unsettled state of trade.'[7] As a result, it was declared that there was, 'no other means left for reducing the people to a manageable and profitable number but emigration.'[8]

In 1828, Paterson compiled a list of 208 families from 67 settlements, marked for removal.[9] The contents of Paterson's list are revealing as he documented the reasons why those on it were singled out for eviction. It is evident that the continued suppression of illicit activities was a factor in Paterson's decision-making process. Many of the individuals listed are identified as being of, 'doubtful character'.[10] Several known illicit distillers and smugglers feature on the removal register. John Bannatine of Slidderie (Sliddery) was listed as being, 'very poor and the greatest blackguard in Arran.'[11] Robert Armour's account books reveal that Bannatine was heavily involved in disreputable dealings having purchased a pot still costing £4 12s 6d in 1815, in addition to smuggling distilling apparatus across the Kilbrannan Sound for his neighbour William Jamieson in 1813.[12]

Additionally, of the families listed for removal, 94 inhabited crofts at the south-end, the heartland of the island's illicit whisky enterprise. It is therefore apparent that the eviction plans, in addition to reducing the population to a profitable number, served the purpose of fully eradicating illicit practices. The Duke of Hamilton had previously threatened convicted distillers with eviction, decreeing that, 'Those persons detected illegally distilling of Grain must quit my farms as soon as may be.'[13] It was becoming an increasingly accepted belief amongst 'improvers', including Paterson and Brown, that smuggling and unlicensed whisky production produced lazy tenants who refused to co-operate in economic progress. Brown asserted that, 'I think that a man who is a smuggler, as he must leave his lawful occupation, sit up at night, and go about skulking in the day, is not capable of performing the ordinary duties of a farmer; the facility with which he gets spirits to consume himself naturally hurts his constitution ...'.[14] Noted reformer, William Aiton, argued in 1816, that improvement schemes, including forced removals, would produce industrious tenants and prevent islanders, '... lounging half idle and but half fed on their ill-managed farms, or smuggling whisky at the hazard of their lives.'[15]

As the wider island economy faltered in the face of the loss of critical sources of income and employment, agents of the Hamilton estate were able to justify the removal of some of the poorest and most troublesome members of society. The refusal to renew leases in 1828 dispossessed approximately 1,500 island tenants, allowing Brown and Paterson to fully implement agricultural reforms that they believed would considerably benefit the estate. These evictions effectively ended large-scale clandestine distilling on Arran, combining to remove known illicit distillers and act as a deterrent to the remaining islanders who might be tempted to fire up their small stills.

Kilmory minister, Angus McMillan, recorded that the evicted families and cottars from the illicit distilling heartland of the south-end, '... emigrated to North America, but by far the greater part of them removed to the towns of Ayrshire.'[16] Here the main perpetrators of unlicensed Arran production would find themselves under greater supervision from the excise authorities. Furthermore, due to the lack of necessary amenities for distilling, including access to fresh water, in the increasingly crowded Lowland urban centres, exiled islanders would have found it almost impossible to produce a spirit that came close to resembling their native 'Arran water'.

The removal of island tenants was also noted by the Kilbride minister, Allan McNaughton, who stated that the population decline was a direct result of:

> ... an extensive emigration to Canada and Chaleur Bay, which took place in 1830; the care taken to prevent any farther splitting down of

possessions; the decline of smuggling, which, at one time, afforded a sort of occupation for a great number of young men; and increased habits of industry in the rising generation, who, instead of following the old practice of loitering half idle at home, go to trades or service in the low country, or engage as sailors in merchant ships.[17]

Undoubtedly, the virtual eradication of illicit distilling and smuggling had dramatic implications for Arran's economic, social and cultural fabric. The decline of this key industry, coupled with the forced removal of 175 families, finally destroyed traditional communal practices on the island. Distilling had played a key role in life on Arran for generations, bringing the community together through enterprise and subversion of the law and its enforcers. Unlicensed production and smuggling allowed traditional economic and social structures to survive on the island longer than on other parts of the Hamilton estate. Robert Brown's actions between 1814 and 1817 were part of a systematic plan to destroy communal practices in the name of improvement. In terms of agriculture, he was successful, effectively abolishing the run-rig system throughout Arran. However, it was not until the Excise finally introduced effective policies in the early 1820s that the duke's agent was able to effectively tackle illicit distillation and smuggling. The virtual eradication of the clandestine whisky industry coupled with agricultural improvements and mass eviction irreversibly destroyed the traditional Arran way of life and dragged its people into the modern age.

15

'OLD' LAGG DISTILLERY

I N OTHER AREAS OF HIGHLAND SCOTLAND the local economy was stimulated by the establishment of successful legal distilling ventures. Speyside, a legendary haunt of smugglers, developed into the most recognisable licensed whisky-producing region in Scotland following the amendments to the excise laws in the 1820s. On Arran, in the early 1800s, there was a concerted effort by the duke and his agents to set up a licensed still to aid the suppression of illicit production. Legal whisky-making had been absent on the island since the closure of the three small distilleries in the wake of duty increases in the 1790s. In 1816, Robert Brown noted that, 'several individuals were toiling to undertake' licensed distilling on the island.[1] They would, however only consider procuring a licence, 'if the smuggling was suppressed ... '.[2]

The following year, when there was considerable ill-feeling between Brown and the excise establishment, the Chairman of the Board, Woodbine Parish, actively encouraged the establishment of a licensed 40-gallon still on the island. Brown, however dismissed the idea, claiming, 'I will have a great difficulty in prevailing on any person to begin a legal establishment both from the present hazard and danger of the property of the first adventures from the ill will of the smugglers and from the prospect of being undersold by them.'[3] Clearly, competition from widespread smuggling and illegal production was a considerable barrier to the formation of a legitimate distilling venture on Arran.

Certainly, Brown and his employer, the Duke of Hamilton, were unwilling to invest a considerable degree of time and capital in such a scheme until the Excise took decided measures to supress illicit activities. Even the dismissal of local excise officers at Brown's request, was not enough to convince the duke to pursue legal distilling with any real commitment.

This was to change following alterations to the excise laws in the early 1820s, and in 1823, the duke instructed his Arran chamberlain, William Paterson, 'to endeavour to make some arrangements with legal Distillers for having Small Stills established in the island ...'.[4] In the same year Robert Brown confidently stated that, 'In the island of Arran we are just now ready to establish a legal distillery, with a view of consuming the barley, and getting the people to give up illicit distillation; we are at this moment in treaty with a gentleman at Glasgow for the purpose.'[5] In 1824, John Richmond, an Ayrshire mason was commissioned to draw up plans for a, 'Distillery proposed to be made at Lamlash.'[6] Rob Douglas was also paid £4 for limestone to be used in the construction of this planned distillery. For undocumented reasons however, the arrangement fell through and the distillery at Lamlash was never built.

Other plans were subsequently made, and in 1825 a legal still was established at the south-end settlement of Lagg. The distillery was incorporated into the existing site of a corn mill and kiln that had been developed on the banks of Torrylinn Water, at the duke's expense, in 1819. Total construction costs amounted to the considerable sum of £397 16s.[7] Previously, there was a small grain mill on the site, which was utilised by the illicit distillers of the south-end for grinding malt. It was recorded, however, in 1804, that this mill was in a state of considerable disrepair, hence the latter re-development in 1819. It was not unusual for mill buildings to be adapted to facilitate legal stills in Highland regions during this period. In 1825, Alexander Kerr MacKay, with financial assistance from local laird Walter Frederick Campbell of Shawfield and Islay, converted a malt mill into the technically advanced Port Ellen Distillery on Islay.

The legal distillery at the Lagg mill site was set up by a co-operative of prominent local residents; Captain Charles McAlister Shannon, Matthew Spiers and John McKinnon under the trading name The Arran Distillery Company. The Duke of Hamilton financially contributed to the venture, by compensating running costs through rent abatements. For instance, when Captain Shannon paid an Arran Distillery Company bill amounting to £39 6s in 1828, the sum was subsequently reduced from his annual rent as a reimbursement from the estate.[8]

Captain Shannon was the son of Neil Shannon and an Arran native, Mary McAlister, daughter of Hector McAlister of Springbank, Brodick. The Shannon family held the lands of Lephenstrath in southern Kintyre. Shannon was born on Arran around 1786, and at the age of 24 he obtained the rank of captain in the Argyll and Bute Militia. In 1820, he took on the tenancy of Bennecarrigan, one of the largest farms in the south-end. Matthew Spiers was one of the Lowland farmers who settled on the island during the reorganisation of Arran land in 1814-15. A year prior to this, Robert Brown wrote to James McBride, his island associate, informing him, 'Mr Spiers has resolved on going to Arran to look at the island with the view of taking a farm. Be so good as to show him every kind of viability and provide him with a guide to the best parts of the island.'[9] Spiers ultimately settled at Clachaig, obtaining a lease of this considerable agricultural holding which neighboured Bennecarrigan. The modern-day Lagg Distillery site is located on the farmland of Clachaig. The third partner in the venture was the local innkeeper, John McKinnon, who also held the lease of the recently developed Lagg Mill site which facilitated the legal still.

This co-operative ownership structure was a common feature in many of the newly established small Highland distilleries that sprang up in the wake of the liberating 1823 Excise Act. Shannon and Spiers leased two of the largest farms on the island; by establishing a licensed distilling business they ensured a legitimate means of disposing of the vast quantities of grain grown on their farms. Furthermore, the production of draff as a by-product in the distilling process would have provided Shannon and Spiers with a high-quality feedstuff for their cattle herds. Effectively, the distillery was an extension of their agricultural businesses, providing a key outlet for the produce of their holdings with distilling offering a far better potential return than selling grain to mills or other outlets.

As the proprietor of the Lagg Inn, McKinnon would have played a key role in the sale and distribution of the legal distillate. While his involvement provided a tied local market for the Lagg whisky, the spirit was also sold into the Ayrshire market, following the trade patterns established by the Arran smugglers. It was documented in 1834 that licensed Arran whisky, ' ... finds a ready conveyance to the main land, and the towns on the shores of the Firth of Clyde.'[10]

In terms of size, the Lagg distillery was a relatively small operation, equipped with two stills, a 182-gallon (827-litre) wash still and a spirit still with the capacity of 62 gallons (282 litres).[11] Whisky was produced solely from malted bere, allowing the distillery to benefit from the newly introduced malt drawback scheme. Between October 1827 and October 1828, Lagg Distillery claimed £351 11s 11d in malt drawback.[12] It is likely that malting was carried out at the farm steadings of Bennecarrigan and Clachaig. The building reputed to have served as the malt barn and grain store for the distillery still stands on the roadside opposite Clachaig Farm. The malted grain would then have been transported to the mill at Lagg, for grinding. The

The malt barn at Clachaig Farm which served as the grain store for 'Old' Lagg distillery. *Courtesy of the author.*

A rare view of the 'Old' Lagg distillery building from the early 20th century. Following the failure of both the distillery and the later flax works, the structure was converted into a domestic dwelling. *Courtesy of Stuart Gough.*

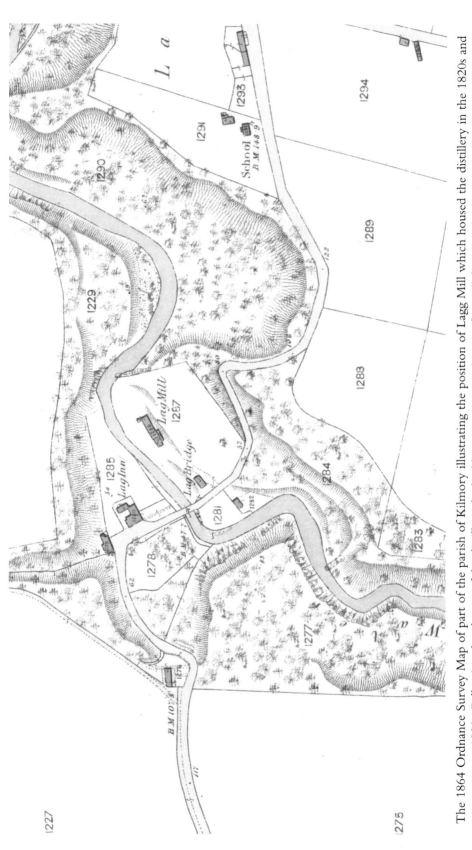

The 1864 Ordnance Survey Map of part of the parish of Kilmory illustrating the position of Lagg Mill which housed the distillery in the 1820s and 1830s. Following the closure of the distillery the building was converted into a flax mill for a brief period in the 1860s.

Reproduced by permission of the National Library of Scotland.

An amusing sketch from *East of Arran* by Boyd Scott showing the altercation between the gauger and the notorious smuggler Dan Cook. *Courtesy of the author.*

The cottages at Balliekine, c.1900. Here, in the late 19th century, the Sillars siblings had a notable run-in with the excise authorities. *Courtesy of Arran Heritage Museum.*

The remnants of the Lochranza illicit still site which was in use as recently as the early 1940s. Situated behind the Anchorage, all that remains of the site are some bottles and fragments of copper. *Courtesy of the author.*

The 'Smuraig Sma' Still' site as discovered by Rab Logan of the Forestry Commission. Secluded in a hollow, the bothy is ideally situated for illicit whisky-making with a ready supply of fresh water flowing from the Arran hills. *Courtesy of the author.*

Lagg Distillery takes shape, 24 October 2018. The images on this page and the subsequent ones were all taken by long-standing Arran 'White Stag' Andrew Smith.
All images courtesy of Andrew Smith.

The modern distillery stands directly above the natural harbour at Cleats from which 'Arran Water' was shipped to the Ayrshire coast during the heydays of smuggling.

The organic design of the new distillery mirrors the illicit whisky bothies of the south-end which blended seamlessly into the island landscape.

The foreshore view beneath the distillery with Ailsa Craig prominent on the horizon.

The stills, manufactured by Forsyths of Rothes, are installed.

Torrylinn Water, which drove the mill, would have provided the distillery with the water required for mashing and distilling. In addition to the two copper stills, the distillery was equipped with a mashtun and washback, both made from wood of either larch or black birch. The stills would have also been charged with wash and low wines from wooden charging vessels. The painting of Lochgilphead Distillery in Argyll, by Sir David Wilkie from 1819, provides a suitable impression of the interior of the Lagg Distillery. Both licensed operations were of similar size, with a comparatively small output in the 1820s.

In line with amendments to the 1823 licensing legislation a spirit safe would have been installed and an excise officer stationed on site to police production. Between 1826 and 1832 William Robertson, James Black, John Hunter, J Buchanan, Henry MacDough, John Hamilton, James McKay, John McPherson, and Benjamin Crabb, were listed as the excise overseers at Arran's only legal still.[13] Licensed distillers were required to provide officers with accommodation in cases where the distillery was situated more than a mile from a market town. The role of the excise officers was to prevent fraud at legal distilleries by ensuring that the correct amount of tax was paid on the volume of spirits distilled. The excise officers were often diligent in the exercise of their duty as McAlister Shannon & Co found to their cost in 1828, when they were fined £25 for breaching regulations.[14] Additionally, the permanent presence of excisemen in the heartland of illicit Arran production would have further inhibited the actions of smugglers.

During the first year of production the distillery manufactured 4,784 gallons (21,748 litres) of malt whisky from 49,144 gallons (223,413 litres) of wash.[15] The following year Matthew Spiers left the business and was replaced by his teenage son, John. Production continued on an upward trajectory with output reaching 6,105 gallons (27,754 litres) in 1828, distilled from 4,308 bushels (approximately 107 tonnes) of malted bere.[16] The following August, however, the distillery ceased production and the company was dissolved by mutual consent in March 1830.[17] At this time Captain Shannon was experiencing considerable financial difficulties. It was documented that he was a particularly poor businessman and was beset with monetary troubles throughout his life. In 1819, he had been forced to sell his ancestral lands in Kintyre.

Within two years of managing Bennecarrigan he was being pressed by Robert Brown for non-payment of rent.[18] Eventually, in 1836 he was forced to give up the tenancy with significant debts owed to the Hamilton estate. In the same year, he was called to the Court of Session accused of owing Allan Fullarton of Woodside Crescent, Glasgow the considerable sum of £289 15s 4d.[19] In 1838, Shannon with his wife and nine children, left Scotland aboard the *Christina*. Their destination was Australia, where he was appointed the superintendent of Moleville Station on the Clarence River. Here, Shannon saw out the remainder of his days, passing away in September 1846, aged 60.

Without Shannon's involvement, the distillery re-commenced production in March 1831, under the sole control of the youthful John Spiers. Interestingly, John also took up the lease of Bennecarrigan when Shannon was forced to abandon the property. Unlike Shannon, Spiers was regarded as a, 'good careful tenant.'[20] Nonetheless, he was still a young man with limited experience and knowledge of the distilling industry. Output for the first six months of his tenure was 2,561 gallons (11,642 litres).[21] On average, approximately 100 gallons (455 litres) of whisky was produced each week from 60 bushels (1.5 tonnes) of malt. In the first full year of production following the re-opening the distillery yielded 4,568 gallons (20,767 litres) of whisky.[22] Despite this relatively small output, the Lagg Distillery produced whisky for five to six days a week, all year round, although production was reduced in the summer months. The likely cause of this was the difficulty in obtaining adequate supplies of grain and peat during this time. Traditionally peat was cut in April and May and would not be ready for burning until the autumn months. Peat was the primary fuel source for drying the barley and firing the stills but coal may also have been used as a fuel for heating the stills. It was recorded by the Kilmory minister that, 'a few of the larger farmers who are close upon the shore, and at a distance from the peat-moss, supply themselves partly with coals from the opposite coast of Ayrshire.'[23] As the Spiers family were the largest farmers in the south-end, this suggests that they might have been supplied with coal from the mainland.

In 1833, John was joined in the running of the distilling business by his brother Robert. Under their management output peaked at 5,689 gallons (25,862 litres) in the first year of the partnership, steadily declining thereafter.[24] The exact date of Lagg Distillery's closure is a matter of debate, with numerous contradictory claims. MacKenzie argued that production ceased in 1836, remarking that, 'In 1834 there was one distillery working at Torlin [Lagg], two years later it had closed ...'.[25] Conversely, in a first-hand account from 1837, John Paterson remarked that, 'A legal distillery has been in operation at Torrylin for several years past ...'.[26] In 1840, local minister Angus MacMillan documented that there was, 'a distillery at Lag.'[27] The following year geologist Andrew Ramsay conducted a survey of Arran. During his tour, he noted various geological features, 'to the east of Lag Inn and of the neighbouring distillery...'.[28] From this documentary evidence it can be gathered that Lagg fell silent at some point between 1837 and 1841.

Although no longer operational, the Spiers brothers continued to hold the lease of the distillery building throughout the 1840s, paying a nominal annual rent of £1. In 1855, the distillery was converted into a flax works and the lease transferred to John Kennedy. This venture was ultimately unsuccessful, as it was recorded in the 1860s that Lagg Mill, '... was originally a Distillery but some years ago was converted into a flax mill, but the flax growing on the island failed. The mill is now idle and likely to be turned into cottages.'[29] Eventually it was converted for this purpose and the building that housed the distillery remains standing, known locally as Kilmory House.

Although the legal Arran venture was short-lived and beset with financial difficulties, the whisky produced was documented as being of fine quality. Paterson claimed that Lagg made, 'spirits nearly equal to the famous Arran Water.'[30] His declaration was backed up in an article in the *Magazine of Botany and Gardening*, no doubt experts in whisky matters. It stated that on Arran, 'a spirit not much inferior to that which is dealt in by smugglers, is manufactured ...'.[31]

Essentially, the production methods and techniques of Lagg Distillery did not differ greatly from the practices of illicit Arran producers. In terms of raw materials, both utilised locally sourced barley and the fresh water running from the Arran hills. Peat was the predominant fuel source for drying grain and firing the stills. The stills at Lagg were larger than the ones used by illicit producers, approximately three times the volume. Nonetheless, both legal and unlicensed equipment was professionally made, as illicit producers were supplied by coppersmith Robert Armour of Campbeltown. As was the case with unlicensed Arran whisky, legal spirits were not matured for any considerable period of time. There were no warehousing facilities at Lagg, therefore the distillate would have been conveyed directly to market in wooden casks and consumed soon after production. Perhaps it was the knowledge and experience of the illicit Arran distillers that gave their product the edge over their legal rivals. In any case, the whisky produced by both sets of distillers would be deemed almost undrinkable in relation to modern tastes.

Lagg distillery was a very small venture operating in an increasingly commercial and competitive market. At the time of Lagg's closure neighbouring Campbeltown had developed into an established centre of legal distilling. Between 1823 and 1837, 27 distilleries were built in the town, the largest of which had an annual output of 25,000 gallons (113,652 litres) of whisky.[32] This Kintyre town had considerable production and communications advantages over Arran with a natural sheltered harbour which facilitated large vessels and supported the herring fisheries. This enabled regular steam packets to operate between Campbeltown and Glasgow, as well as the coastal towns of Ayrshire.

As a result, distillery companies were able to rapidly ship their whisky to the Lowland markets and beyond. Lagg continued to be hampered by poor transport links. It was recorded by the Kilmory minister in 1840 that there were still, '... no harbours; at least none which a vessel can enter, except at high water, and the largest of them will not, even then, admit vessels of more than fifteen tons.'[33] In terms of internal communication, the bridge over Torrylinn Water at Lagg was not constructed until 1828, cutting off the distillery from the small harbour at Cleats when the burn was in spate. Furthermore, Campbeltown boasted the only workable coal deposits in the Western Highlands, significantly lowering production costs for the town's distillers.

On Islay, there was a similar boom in production, where the number of distilleries doubled from six to 12 between 1823 and 1830.[34] Distillery companies were attracted by the pure water, large quantities of barley grown on the island and vast peat reserves. All Islay distilleries also undertook their own malting. For the coastal distilleries such as Lagavulin and Ardbeg, access to the sea was literally on their doorsteps. Legal Arran production was unable to compete with the rising number of larger distilleries in neighbouring districts, which were able to exploit numerous infrastructural advantages. MacKenzie summarises that legal distilling and other small Arran industries were inhibited by geographical location and the development of technically advan-taged, large-scale manufacture:

> ... in time the competition of the great manufacturing centres was bound to close the doors of humbler and more expensive local estab-lishments, handicapped as these were, too by difficulties of access.[35]

At the time of Lagg's closure, eight other Highland distilleries ceased production. Brian Townsend argues that the main reason behind the failure of these small Highland distillers was the simple fact that there were too many distilleries, producing too much whisky, flooding the market and making small-scale production unviable.[36] For every new firm that succeeded, dozens failed.

The actions of the large Lowland distillers compounded the over-production problems of the industry. The Haigs and Steins, two significant distilling families, invested heavily in developing new equipment, allowing them to produce vast quantities of legal whisky in a short time. By the early 1830s, eight Lowland distill-eries were annually producing over 100,000 gallons (454,609 litres) of whisky using enlarged pot stills.[37] By the early 1840s, however, the consumption of spirits in Scotland, which was around 70% malt whisky, slumped from a peak of approximately 6.6m gallons (30m litres) in 1836, to just below 5.6m gallons (25.4m litres) in 1843.[38]

This sharp decrease in whisky sales mirrored the general down-turn in the Scottish economy. In 1835 and 1836, there were wide-spread crop failures throughout the Highlands. In western regions the weather was so wet that it was almost impossible to dry peats, making malting and distilling very difficult. Subsequently, licensed stills ceased production and many were placed on short-term working. As a result the small, under-funded malt distilleries of the Highlands were the most vulnerable to closure. A rise in duty rates of a shilling per gallon of whisky between 1830 and 1840, also lowered the profit margins of these ventures at a time of increased economic uncertainty. These wider economic trends and developments in the Scottish distilling industry made the distillery at Lagg increasingly vulnerable to closure.

In conclusion, Lagg Distillery was unsuccessful due to a number of social and economic factors including a lack of capital, the limited distilling and business experience of the owners, increasing competition from neighbouring regions of distilling activity with better transport links such as Campbeltown and Islay which created difficulty in getting Arran whisky to the Lowland market.

MacKenzie asserted that even the reputation of the old time 'Arran Water', the revered whisky of the smuggling days, could not save the island's only legal still in the face of economic hardships and the changing nature of distilling in Scotland.[39] Ultimately the transition from illicit to legal whisky manufacture on the island was short-lived, ending in complete failure as Lagg fell silent within 20 years of its establishment.

16

THE SMA' STILL RETURNS

THE COLLAPSE OF LICENSED distilling on Arran encouraged the partial recovery of illicit whisky-making and smuggling. The Head of the Board of Inland Revenue, John Wood, stated in the 1850s that the island was displaying, 'Some symptoms of the revival of illicit distillation.'[1] Throughout the 1840s and 1850s there were several widely publicised smuggling incidents. In 1845, Peter Hamilton, James Jamison and Alexander Jamison, were tried at Inveraray Circuit Court, accused of obstructing and deforcing three excise officers.[2]

On 27 December 1843, the officers proceeded to a house occupied by Peter Hamilton, near the farm of Auchenhew (NS 1032140), believing that illicit distilling was being carried out. Upon the approach of the excisemen, the accused barricaded themselves in the house and thrust sharpened pieces of wood underneath the door, injuring officer Dugald Paterson. After the officers abandoned the seizure, the smugglers came out of the house and assaulted John Mathieson, a shoemaker at High Kilmory, who had attempted to assist the gaugers. The three men pelted him with stones and attacked him, landing heavy blows to his chest and shoulders. It was noted that Hamilton had a previous assault conviction. The Auchenhew smugglers were subsequently found guilty, with Alexander Jamison declared a fugitive after failing to appear in court. His two accomplices, Peter Hamilton and James Jamison were sentenced to nine months' imprisonment in Rothesay Jail. Illicit distillers and smugglers regularly frequented this establishment during this time; it was recorded during an inspection of the prison that, 'Smugglers accustomed to the mountain air are sometimes affected by the confinement ... most of them come from the island of Arran.'[3]

In 1851, the Board of the Inland Revenue received information that, 'illicit distillation was carried out to a very large extent in the island of Arran.'[4] Subsequently, the chairman of the board instructed Mr Donald Durran, examiner at London, and Mr Dugald McCraig, assistant examiner at Campbeltown, to lead a party of excise officers and cuttermen to make a thorough search of the island. The *Glasgow Herald* published a detailed report of their efforts, outlining that the excise party searched the south-end for over a week. Initially the officers, 'proceeded to search the hills of Kildonan; this range being intersected by deep valleys, rugged and bold precipices, the officers had great difficulty in reaching the smuggling ground ... they succeeded, after toilsome marching and counter-marching in discovering four bolls of malt in active operation, which was destroyed on the spot.'[5] The following day the same party, 'searched farm-steadings and houses, and about Sliddery they found concealed in a farmer's house in that locality three bolls of malt and a still head.' After the comparatively easy work of inspecting the local settlements the group searched, 'the Rocks of Bennan'. It was stated that, 'these wild and plutonic eruptions are admirably adapted for smuggling purposes and they succeeded in discovering concealed, under the fragmentary masses, six bolls of malt ready for kiln-drying, which was destroyed.'[6] They also located, 'after an agreeable parade, 4 bolls of ground malt,' on the shore of Bennan.[7] The following week a search was conducted of, 'the woods of Balagan,[8] where they found, after much tearing of trousers and flesh among the brushwood and tangled forest, 6 bolls dry malt, which they seized and removed to one of the neighbouring inns.'[9] No doubt the locals would have been thoroughly amused by the officers struggles until their hidden equipment and produce was uncovered by their endeavours. The officers were praised for the, 'firm and gentlemanly manner,' by which they conducted their investigation. The *Herald* was of the opinion that smuggling practices had, 'a most demoralizing influence on the habits of the people. It tends to engender drunkenness, indolence, ignorance and habits of filthiness ...'.[10] The report concluded by predicting that, 'the smuggling trade of our own Island of Arran has received such a check this month as will be the means of its entirely abandoned in time to come.'[11] Certainly, during this latter period smuggling on the island was not as widely practised as it had been in the heydays of the first two decades of the 19th century.

Nonetheless, duty increases throughout the 1850s made illicit distillation attractive to those bold enough to operate outwith the law. In 1855, it was documented that, 'Smugglers have never been entirely extirpated in the Island of Arran and it would appear that the recent great advance in duty has called them into renewed activity.'[12] Despite the continuation of illegal production, Arran whisky was no longer viewed as being of superior quality to the distillate of the large-scale legal distilleries. The *Glasgow Gazette* of 17 January 1852 recorded that:

> For more than half a century the peasantry of the south end of the island have been tempted to prosecute the illicit distillation of whisky, which they maintain is the most remunerative form in which they can dispose of their crops of barley. The spirits produced in these secret manufactories is strong and 'ramp' and not at all equal to the legal production of Islay and Campbeltown, where the leisure, experience, and chemical improvements, have enabled the distillers to produce a finer and much superior liquor. The secrecy, hurry, and terror in which the smuggler must work necessarily has the effect of injuring the quality of his goods ...[13]

Despite its inferior quality, Arran whisky did retain an element of its status and reputation, selling for eight shillings a gallon in the Ayrshire towns.[14] Nonetheless, 'Arran water' increasingly struggled in the Lowland market which was flooded with high-quality legal whisky.

Unlicensed distillers on the island were further inhibited by the conduct of the local revenue officers. Unlike the early decades of the 1800s, the excisemen were rigorous in their actions, employing effective measures to ensure the suppression of illicit activities. The *Glasgow Gazette* recorded that nearly a dozen smuggling bothies located at the south-end were, 'discovered and demolished, and it is now believed that an end has been put to their operations ...'.[15] The gaugers were now actively destroying equipment, a practice that they were unwilling to undertake before 1823. The newspaper further detailed how officers enacted the detections and seizures:

> As it is indispensable that these little distilleries be planted close by a stream or rivulet, the officers had little difficulty in finding them out by tracing the courses of the streams, and watching whether any particles of malt or wash could be found on the margins.[16]

As a result of the rigorous actions of the Excise, islanders implemented measures to camouflage their smuggling bothies:

> Some of them were so thoroughly concealed with heather and bushes that a casual huntsman or tourist would never have suspected their existence, the more active operation being carried on at night.[17]

The proactive actions of local officers illustrates that whilst illicit distilling was eradicated in many Highland regions of Scotland, Arran remained a problematic area for the Excise. Illicit distillation was, however, dwindling on the island. Unlicensed activities became concentrated in a few small and isolated farms on the southern coastline, where they were carried out by a few dedicated smugglers. Clashes between these staunch islanders and the increasingly committed excisemen were not uncommon in the latter half of the 19th century. It was claimed that, 'The lower classes of inhabitants ... are prepared when occasion offers to maintain their right to illicit distillation by force.'[18] The Bennan and Kildonan regions, particularly the settlement of Craigdhu, were notorious for illegal production during the 1850s. In 1855 Mr Henry Evans, preventative officer of the island revenue, detailed the brutal manner in which he and his party were assaulted at this south-end steading:

> I beg leave to inform you of a most desperate attack made upon me and the men under my command at a place called Craigdhu, south end of this island ... In searching one of the houses there we found four bags of malt; and in endeavouring to remove or destroy it, we were surrounded by a number of persons inside the house, in a narrow passage, and beaten and abused. I saw distinctly that I could not effect my object without loss of life, and decided on despatching one of my men for the Coastguardsmen at Lamlash, leaving then only one man and myself. In about one hour after he had left they renewed the attack, dragged us, by superior numbers, outside, beat and knocked us down several times, and ultimately carried us into the house of James Stewart, farmer, there; and, when inside, renewed the attack. I may add that Stewart is brother to the person in whose house the malt was found. The above case has been reported to the proper authorities, and no doubt the parties will be brought to justice, as all of them are well known and desperate smugglers. I have endeavoured to give a sketch of what occurred, but it falls short of the real character of the attack. I may also add that, on medical examination, one of my ribs is broken, my sides are black and blue, and my hands desperately cut. The men are also much injured.[19]

The following March, Donald Cook, Duncan Cook, Marion Stewart, and Mary Stewart (née Currie), were tried at the Inveraray Circuit Court, accused of the outrage against Evans and his men. The Cooks were labourers at neighbouring Shannochy Muir, whilst Marion Stewart was employed as a grocer and tobacco dealer. It was determined that the officers entered

Marion Stewart's house and tried to open a locked door. During this the officers were confronted by the accused smugglers. Unfortunately for the excisemen, the presiding judges, Lord Cowan and Lord Deas declared that Evans, in his capacity as an excise officer, was not entitled to force open locked doors without a warrant. Therefore, the resistance of their assailants was not unlawful and the islanders were acquitted of all charges.[20]

The islanders may have won this round but, Evans and his associates were determined to enact revenge and catch the south-end distillers in the act. In 1858, Evans was involved in another violent struggle, documented in the *Glasgow Herald*:

On Tuesday week ... a sensation was created in the Island of Arran. The active and resolute officer of the preventative service, Mr. Evans, and his two assistants, Andrew McMillan and Murdoch Mathieson, on the morning of that day made a seizure at Port-Bennan, before dawn of morning. In a wild and dangerous place of the coast, they descried what turned out to be a temporary bothy, fixed over the rock. Mr. Evans, leaving his assistants above, slung himself down into the midst of the party, when he was immediately knocked down by one of the smugglers, but quickly seizing his musket, with the butt and he knocked over his assailant, who staggered and rolled over and down the precipitous incline of the hill to about 100 feet. The other parties meanwhile made good their escape. The assistants, McMillan and Mathieson, jumped after the man who had been stunned by Evans' blow. Some blank shots were fired at the others, but the only one taken was the smuggler Cook, who had been rendered faintish by the blow from the musket of the officer. The others, meanwhile, though escaping, cannot elude the vigilance of the preventatives. In the bothy were found all the apparatus used in the making of whisky. The copper still-head and worm were taken to Lamlash, and a considerable quantity of wash and feints was destroyed upon the spot. The prisoner was taken to Rothesay jail, where, we learn, he suffers an incarceration of three months. It must be allowed that ever since the increased duty has been placed upon the spirits the temptation to illicit distillation has, in proportion, greatly increased; and in such places as the wild hills of Arran, where the chances of detection, from the remoteness of the dwellings, are lessened, the pains and penalties of the law are braved, though the risk run is very great where such activity is found in the officers of the service. Doubtless this detection will act as a beneficial warning to others who may contemplate incurring such risks.[21]

On this occasion, the excisemen clearly got the upper hand and the island smugglers were left to regret the loss of their valuable equipment and, in the case of the unfortunate Cook, his liberty. Interestingly, the *Glasgow Herald* documented the alleged reasoning for the actions of Cook and his fellow clandestine distillers. They reported that, 'on this occasion one of the parties implicated was soon to have been married, and that the preliminary manufacture of "aqua vitae" was to give éclat to the hymeneal ceremonies – the social and genial influences of the "fiery god" being deemed an almost indispensable requisite to prolong the festive moments and bacchanalian enjoyments.'[22] At this time Arran 'peatreek' was predominately produced for local consumption at social gatherings as the smuggling of it to the mainland had long since ceased being a viable source of income and employment on the island. Its profitability had been eroded by the higher quality and greater demand for legal whisky, coupled with the constant vigilance of the excise officers and the heavy penalties enforced by local magistrates.

Latterly, Arran smugglers were increasingly involved in the inward trafficking of whisky from the mainland. In 1859, John Innes, master and owner of the *Endeavour of Arran* and John Taylor, a seaman on the boat, were accused of stealing 3½ gallons of whisky from a cask on board a vessel belonging to Messrs James Harvey & Co, wine and spirit merchants from Paisley. The *Glasgow Free Press* recorded that, 'it appeared that the whisky and several barrels of ale had been shipped on board the *Endeavour* for the purpose of being conveyed to the Island of Arran.'[23] The stolen cargo did not make it very far however, as the *Endeavour* was found, 'adrift in the harbour, and on the vessel ... the skipper and his mate were found in a helpless state of intoxication, with a jar of whisky and a gimlet lying beside them.'[24] The inebriated pair clearly struggled to live up to their vessel's name, and were convicted of smuggling as the remaining contents of the jar corresponded to the strength and flavour of the whisky in the tampered cask. Both were subsequently sentenced to 30 days in prison, providing them with plenty of time to recover from their exertions. The rise in the import of whisky confirmed that any illicit distilling on the island was no longer capable of supplying the local market.

In 1860, one of the last detections of large-scale illicit manufacture occurred on Arran. The *Glasgow Herald* reported the following from the Rothesay JP Court:

> Archibald McKinnon, residing at Sliddery, in the parish of Kilmory, Arran, was brought before Provost McEwen and Bailie Brown today, at the instance of Anthony Rodgers, supervisor, Greenock, charged with having had in his possession several articles used in the distillation of spirits. Mr Stewart, Inland Revenue officer, deponed to having found, in McKinnon's house, in ingeniously constructed places of concealment, a still head and worm, about 15 gallons of fermented wash, a tun and worm-tub, and a few casks and jar – some of which articles appeared to have been very recently used. McKinnon failed to appear and, being found guilty, was amerced [sic] in penalties amounting to £2,100. This seems to have been a case of systematic smuggling, as McKinnon, according to the evidence, had everything for carrying on distillation except the still.[25]

The exorbitant fine imposed on McKinnon provides clear evidence of the perilous nature of smuggling on the island after 1823. Those caught faced either imprisonment or financial ruin. In the end, it was not worth the effort and by the late 19th century the suppression of the illicit whisky industry on Arran was complete. Unlicensed distilling was squeezed into oblivion by a combination of the improvement movement, excise reform and the emergence of an increasingly commercialised legal whisky industry. It is fitting that the traditional stronghold of the south-end offered the final resistance to the eradication of the illicit island economy. Nonetheless, despite ferocious resistance from Arran residents for over half a century, the Excise had won the battle as unlicensed distilling on a significant scale became a remnant of the past.

17

'ARRAN WATER' TODAY

I N THE LATE 19TH CENTURY, home distilling, a traditional craft that had been practised on the island for
centuries, was a dying art. Like the Gaelic way of life, it had
been systematically destroyed by the actions of perceived outsiders
and their strategies for improvement and economic development.
Nonetheless, in the face of great adversity, some islanders held on
to their distilling traditions and passed their knowledge onto
future generations. There is substantial oral evidence to suggest
that in times of shortage and celebration, stills were fired and illicit
Arran whisky continued to flow into the late 19th century and
throughout the 20th. Furthermore, various folk tales have been
recorded that demonstrate the tradition of small-scale distilling
and islanders outwitting the Excise during this latter period.

MacKenzie documents a story from the 1860s, when three
casks of whisky were seized by excisemen on the shore below
Lagg. Whilst guarding their prize, the officers were approached by
the brother of the Lagg innkeeper, who invited them to join him
for some liquid refreshment. Unwisely, they accepted his offer
and abandoned the casks on the shore. When they returned, they
found them filled with seawater, the whisky having been run-off
into washing tubs by the locals and carted beyond the reach of
the law.[1]

Many of these smuggling fables were embellished by the
historians and travel writers of the early 20th century who interviewed elderly Arran tenants. Boyd Scott in, *The East of Arran*,

romantically recalls the tale of Dan Cook, a notorious illicit distiller and smuggler from Largybeg, south of Whiting Bay. It was said that Cook worked his sma' still on the bank of the burn close to his house. One day, the Revenue Cutter landed a search party nearby without warning, leaving Dan with no time to hide his incriminating materials. Two of the crew converged on the Cook household. There was a central passageway through the house and a gauger made for each entry, cutting off the Arran man. Nonetheless, Cook was not going to surrender his precious equipment without a fight. As each exciseman attempted to open the door, he found a threatening hay fork barring his path. Little did they know that Cook was alone in the steading, holding the two forks cunningly tied together by the shanks. Believing they required assistance, one of the men went in search of his colleagues, leaving the other guarding the settlement. Dan, subsequently launched himself out of the house and restrained the remaining officer, tying him, 'like a sheep hand and foot.'[2] He then disposed of the gauger in a hole in the peat stack.

Commonly, throughout the Highlands, tales are told of equipment and casks hidden in peat stores to avoid detection; this is, perhaps, the only incident where an exciseman was concealed in such a manner. With the gauger tied up, Cook was able to conceal his compromising utensils in a cave on the shore. Shortly afterwards, the other officer returned, supported by the rest of the Revenue Cuttermen. Unnerved by the disappearance of their comrade, they instructed Dan to surrender and fired a warning volley over the house. Unperturbed, Dan made his appearance, claiming to know nothing of the missing officer. Eventually, the cries of their lost companion brought the crew to the peat stack. Cook claimed that the wee folk must have tied up the officer or perhaps the man had sought a quiet place for a smoke and had got himself in a tangle. After recovering their colleague, the antagonised crew carried out a thorough search of the area hoping to discover anything that would incriminate Cook. Nothing was found however, and the crew left for their ship in a demoralised state.[3]

Boyd Scott's version has undoubtedly been fictionalised, with certain elements exaggerated to add to the excitement. Nonetheless, a similar account of Dan Cook single-handedly holding off two excisemen, and depositing one in a peat stack, was documented by MacKenzie, several years prior to Scott's adaptation.[4] This suggests that there is a degree of legitimacy to the tale, based on the exploits of the Arran smugglers from the 19th century. Certainly, the Cook family were highly active in various distilling and smuggling exploits. Excise records show that Finlay Cook was a renowned island smuggler, having vessels and whisky seized on numerous occasions in the 1820s. Furthermore, Daniel Cook had a notable run in with the Excise, breaking an officer's leg in 1807 (see page 26).

Although these tales are grounded in truth, it must be remembered that they have been altered over the centuries by generations of islanders to promote the local smugglers as the 'heroes' of the stories, battling against the hated and incompetent excisemen. Their recollections were subsequently edited by numerous 20th-century writers to make their own books more interesting and exciting. The renowned Scottish dramatist, Robert McLellan, also used the stories of Arran whisky trafficking as inspiration for his 1938 play, 'The Smuggler' which details the adventures of Jamie Hamilton escaping the clutches of the gaugers with a little help from the cunning local doctor. These parables are thoroughly entertaining and enjoyable, in addition to being of great value to the narrative of distilling and smuggling on Arran. The folk tales and dramatisations highlight that distilling customs and traditions survived long after the collapse of the illicit and legal industry in the 1840s and 1850s. Distilling remained a key element of the island's culture and identity, kept alive by the storytellers of the early 20th century.

The survival of Arran whisky production was also ensured by a number of small home distillers from this period. Oral evidence suggests that unlicensed production on a very small scale continued in isolated regions of Arran. Liz Dale, a resident of the north-end, remembers her great uncle, Jock Henderson, showing her brother, Angus Stewart, the location of an old still in the 1950s near the settlement of Balliekine (NR 870396), on the north-west coast of Arran. Unfortunately, it was deemed inappropriate for her to tag along as she was a young girl at the time, therefore the exact location of this illicit enterprise remains unknown. Liz explained that the still was operated in the 1880s and 1890s by Shaunie Sillars and his sister Mary.

Liz also remembers visiting Mary Sillars at her croft in Balliekine as a child and she recounted the tale of Shaunie and Mary's encounter with the Excise in the late 1880s. Allegedly, Shaunie was working the still by the burn above High Balliekine when he spotted the Revenue Cutter landing a small boat on the shoreline below. He signalled to Mary at the croft, warning of the approaching excisemen so that she could conceal the 'peatreek' that was being stored there. She subsequently stowed the offending liquor in the loft, but was unable to remove the telltale ladder from the trapdoor before the first officer arrived demanding entry. As the foolhardy exciseman barged in and placed his foot on the ladder, Mary seized a large knife from the kitchen table and growled, 'one more step and I'll liberate you.'[5] The tale concludes with the officer having second thoughts about investigating, quickly fleeing the scene and informing his colleagues that he found nothing during his search.

From Liz Dale's recollections, it would appear that there were several stills in operation at Balliekine during this period. Its unique location and circumstances offer part of the explanation for the lingering practice of small-scale distilling. Traditional agricultural methods remained at this northern settlement long after they had disappeared throughout the rest of the island. In 1914, MacKenzie documented that, 'runrig came to a violent end on the Hamilton lands, though it lingered elsewhere a while longer, and may be said to exist at Balliekine.'[6] Until the 1950s, the tenants of Balliekine worked the land on a communal basis, with seven tenants renting and working six shares. This system had remained virtually unchanged since the 1700s. The north-west part of Arran, incorporating Balliekine, was bestowed by the eighth Duke of Hamilton to his illegitimate daughter, Anne, as a dowry when she married Henry Westenra, an Irish aristocrat, in the early 19th century. Thus, Balliekine was left virtually unaffected by the agricultural reforms introduced by the Hamilton estate. As a result, communal activities, including run-rig agriculture and domestic distilling continued to thrive in this isolated Arran clachan until the 20th century. As has been outlined previously, the destruction of the traditional Arran way of life, by improvers such as Robert Brown, greatly influenced illicit distilling and played a key part in its eradication throughout the island. Balliekine was exempt from this interference and the communal structure of the township facilitated the survival of home-distilling traditions into the 20th century.

It is likely that the residents of Balliekine were tempted to fire up their stills following the repeal of the malt tax in 1880. This allowed distillers to buy malted barley, rather than having to make their own which was time-consuming and left them vulnerable to detection. Prior to this, malt could only be purchased from licensed maltsters. This legislative change coincided with a reduction in the number of revenue preventative staff throughout Scotland. This resulted in a resurgence of illicit distillation in the Highlands, particularly in the areas of Inverness-shire, Ross-shire and Sutherland. The Sillars siblings, and one or two others, undoubtedly resurrected unlicensed production in isolated regions of Arran in order to take full advantage of these favourable conditions.

The continuation of illicit production was not solely confined to one settlement on Arran. Kate Hartley, who retired from employment at the Isle of Arran Distillery in 2015, recalled a childhood adventure in the late 1950s when she discovered an old still site behind the Anchorage in Lochranza. She remembers finding, 'a bit of a stone dyke, there were jars, pots and bottles all lying about, it was a bit like a wee house.'[7] After finding the structure she informed her great aunts who told her that she, 'was never ever, ever to go up the hill behind the house again because there was a bad man up there.'[8] Kate recalls that after she reported her findings, the house gardener, Jimmy Stronach, was sent to destroy what remained of the still. This old still was probably in use during the late 1930s and early 40s, when there was a great shortage of whisky due to the depression years and World War II.

Sma'-still whisky continued to be produced for local consumption into the latter half of the 20th century. Kate Hartley's husband, John, recounted being offered a dram of home brew at a wedding at Moss Farm in 1967: 'I will always remember looking at it and I thought it looked awful cloudy and I'm sure there were still wee bits of corn floating in it.'[9] Allan Little, a resident of Lamlash, recalled tasting locally made whisky in the late 1970s, asserting that, 'it nearly blew ma head off when he gave us a wee tipple.'[10] The spirit was made by one of the maths teachers at Arran High School who had a small pot still in his house at Murray Crescent. Charles MacLean, the Edinburgh-based whisky writer and connoisseur, detailed his experience of sampling unlicensed Arran whisky:

My formative years were spent at Kildonan on the south coast of Arran, where we have a family cottage. As late as 1972, I tasted whisky allegedly made locally, and I have to say it was horrible. Ian Colquhoun and a local gamekeeper, Ronnie MacDonald, had a lemonade bottle of the stuff at The Glen Farm, a very remote place at the back of Kildonan. A local farmer, Lordy MacDonald, joined us, and when he saw the bottle he insisted on trying it. He filled a glass and knocked it back as though it was normal whisky, but of course it was over strength, and within a couple of minutes of drinking it, he'd passed out. Next day he was mowing Whiting Bay golf course, and he kept falling off the tractor, literally falling off it.[11]

There was also a home-made still operating in Corrie in the early 1980s. It was constructed and worked by a well-known resident of Corrie Terrace, who stashed it in the whin bushes of the nearby quarry. Mark Bunyan recalls sampling the home-distilled spirit as a young man. He remembers the liquor being, 'crystal clear and when I took a nip it filled my whole chest with heat ... I could feel it behind my eyes.'[12] Mark also detailed that a quarter bottle of the home-brew was delivered to another Corrie resident, Willie Stewart. He was not seen for three days afterwards. Fortunately, a concerned local went round to check on him, and found him conscious, albeit looking rather the 'worse for wear.' Not long after this incident, the Corrie Hotel darts team were travelling to the Kinloch Hotel for an away league match. A half-bottle of the locally made spirit was taken for the journey. By the time the team arrived in Blackwaterfoot, the bottle was empty and the eight-man team, with the exception of the driver, were virtually incapacitated. Unsurprisingly, they were well beaten, with many of them struggling to see, never mind hit, the dart board. Local publican, Lawrence Crawford, was apparently furious at the events, declaring that the home-brew was 'ruining his profits.' According to Mark, after this the still 'became legendary in Corrie.'[13] Unfortunately, the local police sergeant was informed of the goings-on and had a quiet word with the perpetrator who disposed of the still soon afterwards.

In terms of licensed production, after an absence of almost 160 years, legal spirit flowed once again on Arran in 1995. The establishment of a whisky distillery at Lochranza was spearheaded by the retired whisky industry veteran Harold 'Hal' Currie after he was inspired by the suggestion of his friend David Hutchison in 1991. In March that year, Hutchison had attended the annual dinner of the Arran Society of Glasgow. At the event the noted Scottish baritone, Peter Morrison, entertained the diners with tales of Arran's rich distilling past. This struck a chord with Hutchison, who had connections to the island, and he suggested joining forces with Currie to create a modern distillery on Arran.

Construction of the Isle of Arran Distillery at Lochranza began in December 1994 and the first distillation took place on 29 June 1995. A small ceremony was held to mark the opening of the distillery on 17 August 1995. In attendance, by personal invitation of Harold Currie, was Lachlan McKinnon, ancestor of William and Donald McKinnon, the smugglers fatally shot by excisemen at Shannochie in 1817. This independent distillery has now flourished into one of the most successful in Scotland. It has a capacity of 1.2m litres of alcohol (316,800 gallons) per annum and attracted over 110,000 visitors for the first time in 2017 while employing 35 members of staff. There is little doubt that the distillery at Lochranza has boosted the modern island economy and it is a key part of Arran's thriving tourism trade, drawing vast numbers of visitors to the north-end of the island. In 2016, the distillery celebrated 21 years since its formation. To commemorate this occasion whisky historian Neil Wilson compiled a comprehensive history of Isle of Arran Distillers Ltd. His work, *The Arran Malt: An Island Whisky Renaissance*, provides a fascinating insight into the inner workings of the company and the development of the distillery at Lochranza.

Sadly in March 2016, Hal Currie passed away just as planning permission for a second distillery to be built by the company was approved.[14] Construction officially started the following year with a small ground-breaking ceremony held on 16 February

2017. The new Lagg Distillery site is situated on the southern coastline, on the farmland of Clachaig, which was worked by the Spiers family throughout the 19th century. Matthew Spiers, and his sons Robert and John, were heavily involved in the establishment and management of the 'Old' Lagg Distillery which lies less than a mile to the east of its modern counterpart. The site offers spectacular views of Kintyre, Ailsa Craig and the Ayrshire coast where 'Arran Water' was enjoyed so readily during the heydays of illicit distillation and smuggling.

This £15-million distilling development will be capable of producing 800,000 litres (176,000 gallons) of spirit each year, a considerable increase from the 25,000 litres once produced annually at 'Old' Lagg Distillery. When fully operational the new venture will increase Isle of Arran Distillers group capacity to two million litres per annum. The three bonded warehouses completed in the spring of 2018 will facilitate the storage of the new Lagg spirit. The distillery will also include a visitor centre and it is estimated that total visitor numbers to both distilling sites on the island will exceed 200,000 by 2020.

Lagg Distillery will be dedicated to the production of a heavily peated malt with a phenolic content of 50ppm (parts per million) mirroring the 'peatreek' crafted in the island's traditional illicit stills. This contrasts with the lighter, un-peated whisky traditionally associated with Isle of Arran Distillers. The decision to focus on peated expressions was made in response to the popularity of the Machrie Moor limited edition range produced at Lochranza. Master Distiller James MacTaggart explained that, 'Having been at capacity at Lochranza for some time, the prospect of starting production at Lagg is extremely exciting. Arran Single Malt continues to grow in popularity – the extra storage alone at Lagg will enable us to lay down more of the award-winning Arran spirit. I'm also very much looking forward to establishing a new style of peated Single Malt at Lagg. By concentrating the distillation of peated malts on the south of the island, I'll also be freed up to create more of our extremely popular limited editions at Lochranza.'[15] James' nephew, Graham Omand, was announced as Lagg's Distillery Manager in May 2018. Having worked under his uncle's guidance at Lochranza for eight years, Graham is ideally suited for overseeing production at the new distillery.

At the time of writing (November 2018) the steelwork of the distillery and visitor centre had been completed. With the structure in place the distinctive shape of the building can be identified. The design was drafted by Ayr-based architects Denham Benn to reflect the mountainous profile of the island. The organic structure, topped with a series of inclined turf roofs, allows the distillery to blend into the surrounding natural environment, in much the same way as the illicit bothies of the south-end merged imperceptibly into the landscape. The copper pot stills arrived at the end of August, the mash tun at the end of September and the traditional wooden washbacks are due to be installed in the winter of 2018 by whisky plant fabricator Forsyths of Rothes. Once this stage has been completed production is expected to start at the end of February 2019, with the grand opening of Lagg Distillery scheduled for later that spring.

Arran whisky has become famous worldwide, firmly putting the island back on the distilling map. The success of Isle of Arran Distillers has created a modern-day whisky revival on the island and the establishment of Lagg Distillery at the south-end brings whisky distilling back to its traditional Arran heartland.

There can be little doubt that this new development will have the same positive impact on the south of Arran as the distillery at Lochranza has had in the north, revitalising this once great whisky-making island.

FOOTNOTES

ABBREVIATIONS

AEO   Arran Estate Office
GCA   Glasgow City Archives
NRAS   National Register of Archives for Scotland
NRS   National Records of Scotland
TNA   The National Archives

INTRODUCTION

1. William McKenzie, *The Book of Arran*, Glasgow, 1914, p.136.

Chapter 1: The Arran Landscape

1. *York Herald*, 1 December 1855.
2. Charles Shore, (2nd Baron Teignmouth), *Sketches of the Coasts and Islands of Scotland, and of the Isle of Man*, London, 1836, p.27.
3. The region of Scotland where the Gaelic language is traditionally spoken. Arran had its own distinct Gaelic dialect which was widely spoken until the beginning of the 20th century. The last native speakers of Arran Gaelic died on the island in the 1990s.
4. MacKenzie, *The Book of Arran*, p.7.
5. *Farmer's Magazine: A Periodical Work Exclusivley Devoted to Agriculture and Rural Affairs*, Vol 18, 1817, remarks in a tour through Arran, p.425.
6. Alistair Gemmell, *Discovering Arran*, Edinburgh, 1990, pp.76-77.
7. John Paterson, *Account of the Island of Arran, Transactions of the Highland and Agricultural Society of Scotland*, Volume 11, 1837, p.154.
8. *Magazine of Botany and Gardening, British and Foreign*, Vol 2, 1834, p.101.

Chapter 2: *Uisge Beatha* and Early Excise Legislation

1. Exchequer Rolls 1494–95, cited in Thomas Dickson (ed.), *Accounts of the Lord High Treasurer of Scotland*, Edinburgh, 1877, p.ccxiv (footnote).
2. Martin Martin, *A Description of the Western Islands of Scotland*, London, c.1695, p.255.
3. John Strawhorn, *The History of Ayr: Royal Burgh and County Town*, Edinburgh, 1989, pp.43-44.
4. Act of Excyse, 1644, cited in Gavin D. Smith, *The Secret Still: Scotland's Clandestine Whisky Makers*, Edinburgh, 2002, p.1.
5. NRAS2177 Bundle 6043: *Tenants of the Island of Arran to James Stewart, Chamberlain of Arran*, 20 February 1759.

6. Neil Wilson, *The Arran Malt: An Island Whisky Renaissance*, Castle Douglas, 2016, p.12.
7. Smith, *The Secret Still*, p.2.
8. Michael Moss & John Hume, *The Making of Scotch Whisky: A History of the Scotch Whisky Distilling Industry*, Edinburgh, 1981, p.38.
9. Smith, *The Secret Still*, pp.3-4.
10. Moss & Hume, *The Making of Scotch Whisky*, p.45.
11. MacKenzie MacBride, *Arran of the Bens, the Glens and the Brave*, Edinburgh, 1911, p.51.
12. Ibid.
13. AEO: *John Burrel's Arran Journal, Vol I, 1766-1773*, pp.187-247.
14. Evidence of John Stewart, farmer and innkeeper near Atholl, Distillery Papers, cited in Tom Devine, The Rise and Fall of Illicit Whisky-Making in Northern Scotland c. 1780-1840, *The Scottish Historical Review*, Vol 54 (158), 1975, p.160.

Chapter 3: The Arran Smuggling Network

1. Wilson, *The Arran Malt*, p.12.
2. Sir Walter Scott, *Heart of Midlothian*, Oxford, 2008, p.8.
3. GCA CE73/1/4: *Rothesay Outport Letter Book: Collector to the Board, 21 March 1822.*
4. MacKenzie, *The Book of Arran*, p.139.
5. Ibid, p.138.
6. Ibid, p.132.
7. GCA CE73/2/3: *Rothesay Outport Board's Orders: Board to the Collector, 11 January 1799.*
8. GCA CE82/1/19: *Campbeltown Outport Letter Book: Collector to the Board, 18 September 1807.*
9. *Edinburgh Advertiser*, October 1796, cited in MacKenzie, *The Book of Arran*, p.133.
10. AEO: *Account of Expenses Laid out by Robert McGregor, 30 September 1808.*
11. AEO: *Petition of Daniel Currie, Sliddery, 12 October 1807.*
12. GCA CE82 1/19: *Campbeltown Outport Letter Book: Collector to the Board, 17 November 1807.*
13. John Burrel cited in, MacKenzie, *The Book of Arran*, p.181.
14. MacKenzie, *The Book of Arran*, pp.129-30.

Chapter 4: The Rise of Illicit Distilling

1. William Murray, cited in, MacBride, *Arran of the Bens, the Glens and the Brave*, p.51.
2. MacBride, *Arran of the Bens, the Glens and the Brave*, pp.51-2.

Footnotes

3. The south-end forms part of the parish of Kilmory. Arran being divided into two distinct church parishes in the 13th century. According to Ordnance Survey Name Books from the 1850s, Kilmory parish extended approximately 24 miles in length from Largybeg, near Whiting Bay, in the south, to Lochranza in the north. It encompasses the south-west and north-west coastline of the island. The other parish, Kilbride, 'extends 14 miles in length, and 7 in breath; comprehending the east and north-east part of the island, from Dippen on the south to the Cock on the north.'

4. Kilmorie, County of Bute, *New Statistical Account*, Vol 5, 1845, p.59.

5. Fifth Report of the Commissioners of Inquiry into the Collection and Management of the Revenue Arising in Ireland; &c. Distilleries, *House of Commons Papers*, Vol 7(405), 1823, evidence of Robert Brown, factor to the Duke of Hamilton, p.170.

6. Fifth Report of the Commissioners of Inquiry into the Collection and Management of the Revenue Arising in Ireland, evidence of Robert Brown, p.168.

7. AEO: *List of Arran Tenants Summoned to Appear at the Excise Court on the 9th, 10th and 12th July 1802.*

8. GCA CE73/1/4: *Rothesay Outport Letter Book: Collector to the Board, 2 March 1816.*

9. AEO: *Macleod Bannatyne, Edinburgh to William Stevenson, Arran Castle, 15 June 1796.*

10. GCA CE73/1/4: *Collector to the Board,* 2 March 1816.

11. *Glasgow Courier,* 3 February 1801.

12. Tidewaiter. A Customs officer who checked goods upon a vessel's landing in order to secure the payment of duties.

13. AEO: *Account of the expense on the seizure of two small casks of whiskie by James McBride, in the Island of Arran, 8th July 1805.*

14. Ibid.

15. Ibid.

16. *Criminal Letters His Majesty's Advocate Against Daniel Cook,* Inveraray Circuit Court, 17 August 1807.

17. *List of Witnesses to be Adducted Against Daniel Cook,* Inveraray Circuit Court, 14 October 1807.

18. Ibid.

19. NRS JC26/1809/37: *Trial papers of Alexander Stewart and Robert Stewart, sons of Donald Stewart, farmer at Largiemenoch [Largiemeanoch], parish of Kilbride, Island of Arran, for the crime of assaulting, beating, and violently maltreating an officer of the Public Revenue, September 1807.*

20. Ibid.

21. Ibid.
22. Ibid.
23. AEO: *Petition of Neil Cook and others, 1806.*
24. *Glasgow Herald,* 11 February 1807.
25. AEO: *Petition of John Robertson, Torbeg, 18 September 1807*
26. NRS CH2/214/2: *Kilmory (Isle of Arran) Kirk Session, Minutes and Poor's Fund Lists,* 16 December 1805, p.41.
27. John Kennedy Cameron, *Gaelic and English Sermons of the Late Rev. John MacAlister, with Memoir,* Inverness, 1897, p.xiii.
28. AEO: *Petition of William Stuart, Benecarigan, 1807.*
29. NRAS2177 Bundle 1010; *Arran estate report to the Duke of Hamilton and Brandon with proposal for reducing the number of tenants on that property, Hamilton Palace, 19 March 1828,* cited in JI Little, Agricultural Improvement and Highland Clearance: The Isle of Arran, 1766-1829, *Scottish Economic and Social History,* Vol 19 (2), 1999, p.142.
30. Smith, *The Secret Still,* p.94.
31. AEO: *The Tacksmen of Benecarrigan to James Lamont, Factor in Arran, 27 March 1809.*
32. AEO: *Copy Memorial and Representation of James Lamont, to the Commissioners of Excise, 1808.*

Chapter 5: The Whisky Makers

1. Robert McLellan, The Smugglers, *Robert McLellan: Playing Scotland's Story,* Colin Donati, (ed.), Edinburgh, 2013, p.391.
2. Fifth Report of the Commissioners of Inquiry into the Collection and Management of the Revenue Arising in Ireland, evidence of Robert Brown, p.171.
3. Cottars formed part of the lower social order of the clachan, occupying a small part of agricultural land in return for labour and services. Some cottars were full-time agricultural workers, but many were part-time tradesmen, such as tailors, shoemakers and weavers.
4. *Declaration of Daniel Cook,* Inveraray Circuit Court, 21 May 1807.
5. Report by Her Majesty's Commissioners for Inquiring into the Licensing System, and Sale and Consumption of Excisable Liquors in Scotland, *Command Papers,* Vol 2, 1860, evidence of Robert Stewart, p.37.
6. AEO: *Petition of John Murphie, West Bennan, 1806.*
7. *Coachan* or *Caochan* is a Gaelic term for fermented liquor or wash.
8. AEO: *Petition of John McCurdy, East Bennan, 15th December 1808.*
9. Fifth Report of the Commissioners of Inquiry into the Collection and Management of the Revenue Arising in Ireland, evidence of Robert Brown, p.167.

10. Dr Samuel Johnson, *A Journey to the Western Islands of Scotland*, London, 1775, p.196.
11. The term 'tacksman' is derived from the Gaelic *daoine uaisle*, which roughly translates to 'gentry' in English.
12. MacKenzie, *The Book of Arran*, p.197.

Chapter 6: Early Legal Distilling on Arran

1. Kilmorie, County of Bute, *Old Statistical Account*, Vol 9, 1793, p.169.
2. William Stevenson to the Collector at Ayr, 19 December 1792, cited in Wilson, *The Arran Malt*, p.15.
3. In comparison, the average volume of unlicensed stills seized throughout Scotland in 1804 was between 25 and 34 gallons.
4. James C Inglis, *Brodick Old and New*, Ardrossan, 1932, p.136.
5. Ibid, p.146.
6. Dr IA Glen, Robert Armour: A Maker of Illicit Stills, *Scottish Studies*, Vol 14, 1970, p.71.
7. AEO: *James and Peter McBride to Captain James Hamilton (Copy), 27 April 1793.*
8. Ibid.
9. Thomas Rees & Rebecca Shaw, *Park Terrace Corn Mill, Lamlash, Isle of Arran: Standing Building Recording and Watching Brief, Data Structure Report,* Rathmell Archaeology, 2005, p.16.
10. Ibid.
11. AEO: *Robert MacGrigor to James McBride, 18 September 1793.*
12. AEO: *Account of Money Lead out by Peter McBride for the Whitehouse Distillery, December 1794–December 1795.*
13. Moss & Hume, *The Making of Scotch Whisky*, p.53.
14. Report Respecting the Scotch Distillery Duties, *House of Commons Papers*, Vol 119, 1798, p.482.
15. MacBride, *Arran of the Bens, the Glens and the Brave*, p.52.
16. Moss & Hume, *The Making of Scotch Whisky*, p.53.
17. AEO: *James and Peter McBride to Captain James Hamilton (Copy), 27 April 1793.*
18. Ardchattan MSS, bundle 86, memorial of the Duke of Argyll and the Justices of the Peace, and the Commissioners of Supply and Heritors of the District of Kintyre etc, relative to the present oppressive state of the Distillery Laws, cited in Moss & Hume, *The Making of Scotch Whisky*, p.53.

Chapter 7: The Making of Arran Peatreek

1. John MacCulloch, *The Highlands and Western Isles of Scotland*, London, 1824, p.372.

2. R Chambers & W Chambers, *The Gazetteer of Scotland,* Edinburgh, 1836, p.56
3. *The Scotsman,* 8 August 1838.
4. *Farmer's Magazine: A Periodical Work Exclusively Devoted to Agriculture and Rural Affairs,* Vol 19, 1818, remarks in a tour through Arran, p.3.
5. Fifth Report of the Commissioners of Inquiry into the Collection and Management of the Revenue Arising in Ireland, evidence of Robert Brown, p.172.
6. Ibid.
7. AEO: *Warrant against John Hendry in Mosend, Hugh MacKenzie Miller at Shedog, Hugh Ker Assistant Miller at Lochranza, and Neil MacCook in Slidery, April 1803.*
8. SW Sillett, *Illicit Scotch,* Aberdeen, 1965, p.86.
9. McCulloch, *The Highlands and Western Isles of Scotland,* p.371.
10. Ibid.
11. Glen, *A Maker of Illicit Stills,* p.77.
12. NRS RH4/42: *Robert Armour, Plumber and Coppersmith in Campbeltown: Account Books, 1811-1817.*
13. Ibid, Vol 3, p.48.
14. Glen, *A Maker of Illicit Stills,* p.78.
15. Ian MacDonald, quoted in Smith, *The Secret Still,* p.43.
16. NRS RH4/42: *Robert Armour: Account Books, 1811-1817,* Vol 2, p.84.
17. Ibid, Vol 1, p.22.
18. Ibid, Vol 3, p.106.
19. Ibid, Vol 4, p.61.
20. Ibid, Vol 3, p.59.
21. Ibid, Vol 1, p.7.
22. MacCulloch, *The Highlands and Western Isles of Scotland,* p.40.
23. Ian Fraser, *The Place-Names of Arran,* Glasgow, 1999, p.142.
24. *Glasgow Herald,* 8 December 1858.

Chapter 8: The Voyage of the Smuggler

1. MacCulloch, *The Highlands and Western Isles of Scotland,* p.372.
2. John McArthur, *The Antiquities of Arran: With a Historical Sketch of the Island,* Glasgow, 1861, p.175.
3. Kilmorie, *New Statistical Account,* p.59.
4. Fifth Report of the Commissioners of Inquiry into the Collection and Management of the Revenue Arising in Ireland, evidence of Robert Brown, p.170.
5. Fraser, *The Place-Names of Arran,* p.126.

Footnotes

6. Robert Buchanan, *The Land of Lorne, Including the Cruise of the 'Tern' to the Outer Hebrides*, London, 1871, p.47.
7. Ibid.
8. GCA CE 82/1/20: *Campbeltown Outport Letter Book: Collector to the Board, 9 May 1808.*
9. GCA CE82/1/31: *Campbeltown Outport Letter Book: J Aubrey, Master of HMS Driver to the Collector (Copy), 16 December 1817.*
10. Kilmorie, *New Statistical Account*, p.57.
11. McArthur, *The Antiquities of Arran*, p.175.
12. *Inverness Courier*, 12 December 1822.
13. Inglis, *Brodick Old and New*, pp.57-8.
14. Chatterton, E Keble, *The Fine Art of Smuggling: King's Cutters Vs Smugglers, 1700-1855,* Tucson, Arizona, 2008, p. 93.
15. GCA CE82/1/27: *Campbeltown Outport Letter Book: Collector to the Board, 8 August 1814.*
16. Kilmorie, County of Bute, *Old Statistical Account,* Vol 9, 1793, p.171.
17. GCA CE82/1/33: *Campbeltown Outport Letter Book: Collector to the Board, 15 September 1819.*
18. GCA CE82/2/29: *Campbeltown Outport Board's Orders: Board to the Collector, 13 September 1816.*
19. GCA CE82/2/29: *Campbeltown Outport Board's Orders: Capt. James Fullarton to the Collector (Copy), 13 September 1816.*
20. GCA CE82/2/29: *Campbeltown Outport Board's Orders: Board to the Collector, 13 September 1816.*
21. *Perthshire Courier*, 6 December 1822.
22. GCA CE82/1/30: *Campbeltown Outport Letter Book: Collector to the Board, 1 July 1817.*
23. GCA CE82/1/30: *Campbeltown Outport Letter Book: Petition of Daniel Kennedy, Alex McKelvie, Allan Bailie and Alex McMillan, Fishermen and Cotters Residing at Whiting Bay in the Island of Arran, now Prisoners in the Tollbooth of Campbeltown (Copy), 1 July 1817.*
24. GCA CE82/1/30: *Campbeltown Outport Letter Book: Mr Anley to the Controller of Customs in Campbeltown (Copy), 1 July 1817.*
25. Ibid.
26. Kilmorie, *New Statistical Account*, p.63.
27. Fifth Report of the Commissioners of Inquiry into the Collection and Management of the Revenue Arising in Ireland, evidence of Robert Brown, p.168.
28. GCA CE82/1/32: *Campbeltown Outport Letter Book: Collector to the Board, 2 August 1819.*

29. Ibid.
30. Ibid.
31. Ibid.
32. Ibid.
33. GCA CE82/2/29: *Campbeltown Outport Board's Orders: Board to the Collector, 18 September 1816.*
34. GCA CE82/1/35: *Campbeltown Outport Letter Book: Petition of Duncan Sillars present prisoner in the Jail of Rothesay (Copy), 11 May 1821.*
35. Ibid.
36. GCA CE82/1/32: *Campeltown Outport Letter Book: Collector to the Board, 2 August 1819.*
37. *Caledonian Mercury*, 22 March 1817.
38. Irvine, County of Ayrshire, *New Statistical Account*, Vol 5, 1845, p.621.
39. *Morning Advertiser*, 23 January 1843.
40. AEO: *Petition of Robert McGrigor, Excise Officer in Rothesay, 25 February 1800.*
41. GCA CE73/1/5: *Rothesay Outport Letter Book: Collector to the Board, 21st March 1822.*
42. Ibid.
43. James Paterson, *Reminiscences of 'Auld Ayr'*, Edinburgh, 1864, p.78.
44. Ibid, p.79.
45. James Paterson, *Autobiographical Reminiscences: Including Recollections of the Radical Years, 1819-1820, in Kilmarnock*, Glasgow, 1871, p.87.
46. Paterson, *Account of the Island of Arran*, p.151.
47. NRS JC26/1811/34: *Trial papers relating to Alexander Kerr senior, farmer or residenter in Kilbride in the Parish of Kilmory on the island of Arran, Alexander Kerr junior, weaver in Kilbride aforesaid, James Nichol or Nicol, weaver, in Kilbride, John Murphy residing in Kilbride and Archibald Cook, farmer, in Shanochy in the Parish of Kilmory for the crime of obstructing, assaulting, deforcing, striking and wounding officers of the Revenue, 6 Sep 1811.*
48. Ibid.
49. Ibid.
50. *Scots Magazine*, Volume 73, 1811, p.792.
51. Paterson, *Reminiscences of 'Auld Ayr'*, pp.81-2.
52. *Chester Chronicle*, 9 August 1805.

Chapter 9: Illicit Whisky Consumption

1. MacKenzie, *The Book of Arran*, p.129.
2. Paterson, *Autobiographical Reminiscences*, p.87.
3. Strawhorn, *The History of Ayr*, p.122.
4. Paterson, *Reminiscences of 'Auld Ayr'*, p.81.
5. Fifth Report of the Commissioners of Inquiry into the Collection and

Management of the Revenue Arising in Ireland, evidence of Robert Brown, p.171.

6. James Hamilton, *Reminiscences of James A. Hamilton; or, Men and Events, at Home and Abroad, During Three Quarters of a Century*, New York, 1869, p.302.

7. NRAS2177 Bundle 1672: *Dr John Stoddart to Robert Brown, 1 November 1816.*

8. AEO: *Rent Ledger: Arran Estate, 1823-1827.*

9. *Evening Chronicle*, 1836.

10. Ibid.

11. *Nairnshire Telegraph and General Advertiser for the Northern Counties*, 23 September 1857.

12. *Glasgow Herald*, 18 February 1881.

13. *Newcastle Journal*, 3 October 1840.

14. NRS CH2/214/2, p.41.

15. Kilmorie, *New Statistical Account*, p.68.

16. Kilbride, County of Bute, *New Statistical Account*, Vol 5, 1845, p.37.

17. Ibid, p.38.

Chapter 10: The Age of Improvement

1. NRAS2177 Bundle 1011: *Brown to Sir MS Stewart, Hamilton Palace, 2 January 1830 (draft)*, cited in Little, *Agricultural Improvement and Highland Clearance*, p. 144.

2. MacCulloch, *The Highlands and Western Isles of Scotland*, p.316.

3. Burrel, quoted in Robert McLellan, *The Isle of Arran*, New York, 1970, p.151.

4. Factor's report of 1800 cited in Campbell, *Arran: A History*, p.135.

5. William Aiton, *General View of the Agriculture of the County of Bute*, Glasgow, 1816, p.81.

6. Ibid, p.viii.

7. MacKenzie, *The Book of Arran*, p.213.

8. *Farmer's Magazine*, Vol 18, 1817, p. 421.

9. Ibid, p.422.

10. John Paterson quoted in Little, *Agricultural Improvement and Highland Clearance*, p.138.

11. MacKenzie, *The Book of Arran*, pp.214-5.

12. Ibid.

13. Little, *Agricultural Improvement and Highland Clearance*, p.138.

Chapter 11: The Crisis of 1815-17

1. NRAS2177 Bundle 1576: *Robert Brown, Hamilton, to the Marquis of Douglas (Draft), 4 June 1812.*

2. Ibid.
3. Fifth Report of the Commissioners of Inquiry into the Collection and Management of the Revenue Arising in Ireland, evidence of Robert Brown, p.170.
4. MacCulloch, *The Highlands and Western Isles of Scotland*, p.316.
5. Fifth Report of the Commissioners of Inquiry into the Collection and Management of the Revenue Arising in Ireland, evidence of Robert Brown, p.168.
6. Ibid, p.169
7. NRAS2177 Bundle 1681: *Robert Brown to Alexander Young, 17 February 1817.*
8. NRAS2177 Bundle 1677: *Alexander Young to Robert Brown, 25 December 1816.*
9. NRAS2177 Bundle 1676: *Alexander Young to Robert Brown, 15 December 1816.*
10. Ibid.
11. NRAS2177 Bundle 1678: *James Davidson to Robert Brown, 8 January 1817.*
12. Fifth Report of the Commissioners of Inquiry into the Collection and Management of the Revenue Arising in Ireland, evidence of Robert Brown, p.169.
13. NRAS2177 Bundle 1675: *Robert Brown to Matthew Brown, Corseflat, Paisley (Copy), 11 December 1816.*
14. NRAS2177 Bundle 1682: *James Davidson to Robert Brown, 2 March 1817.*
15. NRAS2177 Bundle 1679: *Dr John Stoddart to Robert Brown, 19 January 1817.*
16. NRAS2177 Bundle 1682: *James Davidson to Robert Brown, 2 March 1817.*
17. NRAS2177 Bundle 1678: *Dr John Stoddart to Robert Brown, 13 January 1817.*
18. NRAS2177 Bundle 1678: *James Davidson to Robert Brown, 14 January 1817.*
19. Ibid.
20. Ibid.
21. NRAS2177 Bundle 1679: *Dr John Stoddart to Robert Brown, 17 January 1817.*
22. NRAS2177 Bundle 1675: *James Davidson to Robert Brown, 10 December 1816.*
23. Ibid.
24. NRAS2177 Bundle 1680: *Alexander Young to Robert Brown, 15 February 1817.*
25. Ibid.
26. NRAS2177 Bundle 1681: *Robert Brown to Alexander Young, 17 February 1817.*
27. Ibid.
28. Ibid.
29. NRAS2177 Bundle 1681: *Alexander Young to Robert Brown, 22 February 1817.*
30. NRAS2177 Bundle 1682: *Dr John Stoddart to Robert Brown, 19 March 1817.*
31. NRAS2177 Bundle 1683: *Alexander Young to Robert Brown, 25 March 1817.*
32. NRAS2177 Bundle 1681: *Robert Brown to Alexander Young, 17 February 1817.*
33. NRAS2177 Bundle 1678: *Dr John Stoddart to Robert Brown, 13 January 1817.*
34. NRAS2177 Bundle 1680: *Alexander Young to Robert Brown, 15 February 1817.*
35. NRAS2177 Bundle 1680: *James Davidson to Robert Brown, 16 February 1817.*
36. NRAS2177 Bundle 1683: *James Davidson to Robert Brown, 26 March 1817.*

Footnotes

Chapter 12: The Whisky Killings, 25 March 1817

1. *The Scotsman*, 13 September 1817.
2. *Caledonian Mercury*, 11 September 1817.
3. Ibid.
4. Ibid.
5. Ibid.
6. NRAS2177 Bundle 1683: *James Davidson to Robert Brown, 26 March 1817.*
7. Dr R G Thorne, *The History of Parliament: The House of Commons 1790-1820,* London, 1986, p.239.
8. John Pinkerton, *An Enquiry into the History of Scotland,* cited in James Hunter, *Set Adrift Upon the World: The Sutherland Clearances,* Edinburgh, 2015, p.146.
9. Paterson, *Account of the Island of Arran,* p.143.
10. Sir Archibald Alison, *Principles of the Criminal Law of Scotland,* Edinburgh, 1832, p.110.
11. Alison, *Principles of the Criminal Law of Scotland,* p.111.
12. Ibid.
13. *Caledonian Mercury*, 11 September 1817.
14. NRAS2177 Bundle 1683: *Alexander Young to Robert Brown, 31 March 1817.*
15. NRAS2177 Bundle 1677: *Alexander Young to Robert Brown, 25 December 1816.*
16. John Inglis, (ed.), *Dictionary of National Biography,* Vol 29, London, 1892, p.273.
17. Thomas Carlyle & James Anthony Froude, (ed.), *Reminiscences by Thomas Carlyle,* New York, 1881, p.277.
18. *Caledonian Mercury*, 11 September 1817.
19. Ibid.
20. Ibid.
21. Ibid.
22. Ibid.
23. Ibid.
24. Ibid.
25. Ibid.
26. Ibid.
27. NRAS2177 Bundle 1678: *Alexander Young to Robert Brown, 4 January 1817.*
28. NRS JC26/1818/26: *Trial papers of James McBride, now or lately residing at Shanachy, in the parish of Kilmoray, in the west end of the isle of Arran, and Peter McKenzie, now or lately residing at Shanachy aforesaid, and James Nicol, now or lately tailor at Lackievore in the said parish, for the crime of assaulting, obstructing and deforcing officers of the Revenue, 4 May 1818.*

Chapter 13: Excise Legislation in the 1820s

Chapter 13: Excise Legislation in the 1820s

1. Seventh Report of the Commissioners of Inquiry into the Excise Establishment, cited in Devine, *The Rise and Fall of Illicit Whisky-Making in Northern Scotland*, p.176.
2. TNA T1/2301 (15612): *Report on Distilling in Scotland, 1824.*
3. Seventh Report of the Commissioners of Inquiry into the Excise Establishment, cited in Devine, *The Rise and Fall of Illicit Whisky-Making in Northern Scotland*, p.174.
4. Seventh Report of the Commissioners of Inquiry into the Excise Establishment, cited in Devine, *The Rise and Fall of Illicit Whisky-Making in Northern Scotland*, p.176.
5. GCA CE73/1/5: *Rothesay Outport Letter Book: Collector to the Board, 21st March 1822.*
6. Eleventh Report of the Commissioners of Inquiry into the Collection and Management of the Revenue Arising in Ireland, Scotland, *House of Commons Papers*, Vol 13 (389), 1825, p.386.
7. Seventh Report of the Commissioners of Inquiry into the Excise Establishment, evidence of John Anderson, cited in Devine, *The Rise and Fall of Illicit Whisky-Making in Northern Scotland*, p.175.
8. Eleventh Report of the Commissioners of Inquiry into the Collection and Management of the Revenue Arising in Ireland, Scotland, p.385.
9. Ibid, p.386.
10. *Glasgow Herald*, 7 August 1826.
11. Ibid.
12. Twelfth Report of the Commissioners of Inquiry into the Collection and Management of the Revenue Arising in Ireland, Scotland, *House of Commons Papers*, Vol 14 (390), 1825, p.547.
13. Moss & Hume, *The Making of Scotch Whisky*, p.216.
14. Devine, *The Rise and Fall of Illicit Whisky-Making in Northern Scotland*, p.176.
15. *Magazine of Botany and Gardening, British and Foreign*, 1834, p.101.
16. Ibid.
17. Kilmorie, *New Statistical Account*, p.59.
18. Kilbride, *New Statistical Account*, p.26.
19. Paterson, *Account of the Island of Arran*, p.144.

Chapter 14: The Changing Nature of Arran

1. Little, *Agricultural Improvement and Highland Clearance*, p.136.
2. NRAS2177 Bundle 1576: *William Wallace Currie Esquire to Alexander Young (Copy), 22 May 1812.*
3. *Saunders's News-Letter*, 3 November 1821.

Footnotes

4. Fifth Report of the Commissioners of Inquiry into the Collection and Management of the Revenue Arising in Ireland, evidence of Robert Brown, p.168.
5. NRAS2177, Bundle 1010, Paterson to Hamilton, Hamilton Palace, 19 March 1828, cited in Little, *Agricultural Improvement and Highland Clearance*, p.140.
6. Paterson quoted in Little, *Agricultural Improvement and Highland Clearance*, p.140.
7. Ibid.
8. Ibid.
9. Little, *Agricultural Improvement and Highland Clearance*, p.141.
10. Paterson quoted in Little, *Agricultural Improvement and Highland Clearance*, p.142.
11. NRAS2177, Bundle 1010, *Arran estate report to the Duke of Hamilton and Brandon with proposal for reducing the number of tenants on that property, Hamilton Palace*, 19 March 1828, cited in Little, *Agricultural Improvement and Highland Clearance*, p.142.
12. NRS RH4/42: *Robert Armour: Account Books, 1811-1817*, Vol 2, p.44 and Vol 3, p.93.
13. Argyll & Bute Archives, Blain papers, DC6/60/39, letter of Duke of Hamilton to William Stevenson, 8 February 1801, cited in Moss & Hume, *The Making of Scotch Whisky*, p.61.
14. Fifth Report of the Commissioners of Inquiry into the Collection and Management of the Revenue Arising in Ireland, evidence of Robert Brown, p.167.
15. Aiton, *General View of the Agriculture of the County of Bute*, p.355.
16. Kilmorie, *New Statistical Account*, p.57.
17. Kilbride, *New Statistical Account*, p.26.

Chapter 15: 'Old' Lagg Distillery

1. NRAS2177 Bundle 1681: *Robert Brown to Alexander Young, 17 February 1817*.
2. Ibid.
3. Ibid.
4. NRAS2177 Bundle 6163: *Copy Memoranda of Business adjusted with his Grace the Duke of Hamilton of Brandon, Arran Estate, 1823*.
5. Fifth Report of the Commissioners of Inquiry into the Collection and Management of the Revenue Arising in Ireland, evidence of Robert Brown, p.171.
6. AEO: *Accounts of Charge and Discharge for the Arran Estate, 1825*.
7. NRAS2177 Bundle 6163: *Specification of the Corn Miln and Kiln intended to be built at Lag, June 1819*.
8. AEO: *Rent Ledger: Arran Estate, 1826-1833*.
9. AEO: *Robert Brown, Hamilton Palace to James McBride, Arran, 10 April 1813*.

10. *Magazine of Botany and Gardening, British and Foreign*, 1834, p.101.

11. NRS E581/9/53: *Distillery Discharge Vouchers: Argyle South collection: Rothesay: rounds 1-5, 1831-1832.*

12. NRS E581/5/26: *Distillery Discharge Vouchers: Argyle South collection: Rothesay: rounds 5-8, 1827-1828*; E581/6/26: *Distillery Discharge Vouchers: Argyle South collection: Rothesay: rounds 1-4, 1828-1829*; E581/6/27: *Distillery Discharge Vouchers: Argyle South collection: Rothesay: rounds 5-8, 1828-1829.*

13. Ibid.

14. Licensed distillers. Returns of the Number of Licensed Distillers, Informations Laid, and Names and Residences of all Persons Licensed to Distil or Rectify Spirits, who have been convicted in the several Courts of Exchequer, from the 1st January 1827, *House of Commons Papers*, Vol 59 (384), 1828, p.6.

15. Accounts Relating to Distillery from Malt and Raw corn; Duties from Spirits Made in England, Ireland, and Scotland; Beer Made by Licensed Brewers and Victuallers; Spirits Warehoused by Each Distiller in Scotland and Ireland; the Malt Laws, *House of Commons Papers*, Vol 18 (217), 1828, pp 6-7.

16. Malt spirits. A return of the quantity of malt spirits distilled by each distiller, upon which drawback was payable, *House of Commons Papers*, Vol 34 (248), 1831-1832, p.4.

17. *Edinburgh Gazette*, 19 March 1830.

18. NRAS2177 Bundle 6163: *Robert Brown to John Paterson on Captain Shannon's arrears, 11 November 1822.*

19. NRS CS46/1836/1/87: *Decreet, Allan Fullarton Esq v Charles Macalester Shannon and Miss Wortley Stewart Macalester, Jan 1836.*

20. NRAS2177 Bundle 6163: *Report of the Offers given for the following farms on the Estate of Arran, the property of His Grace the Duke of Hamilton and Brandon, Sept 1833.*

21. Seventh Report of the Commissioners of Inquiry into the Excise Establishment, and into the Management and Collection of the Excise Revenue Throughout the United Kingdom. British spirits: part II, *Command Papers*, Vol 30 (8), 1835, p.101.

22. Seventh Report of the Commissioners of Inquiry into the Excise Establishment (British Spirits, Part II), p.101.

23. Kilmorie, *New Statistical Account*, p.68.

24. Seventh Report of the Commissioners of Inquiry into the Excise Establishment, (British Spirits, Part II), p.100.

25. MacKenzie, *The Book of Arran*, p.237.

26. Paterson, *Account of the Island of Arran*, p.152.

Footnotes

27. Kilmorie, *New Statistical Account*, p.56.
28. Andrew Ramsay, *The Geology of the Island of Arran from Original Survey*, Glasgow, 1841, p.55.
29. *Buteshire Ordnance Survey Name Books, 1855-1864*, p.155.
30. Paterson, *Account of the Island of Arran*, p.152.
31. *Magazine of Botany and Gardening, British and Foreign*, 1834, p.101.
32. Seventh Report of the Commissioners of Inquiry into the Excise Establishment, (British Spirits, Part II), pp.100-1.
33. Kilmorie, *New Statistical Account*, p.63.
34. Moss & Hume, *The Making of Scotch Whisky*, p.77.
35. MacKenzie, *The Book of Arran*, p.237.
36. Brian Townsend, *Scotch Missed: The Lost Distilleries of Scotland*, Castle Douglas, 2000, p.23.
37. Moss & Hume, *The Making of Scotch Whisky*, p.79.
38. Ibid, p.88.
39. MacKenzie, *The Book of Arran*, p.237.

Chapter 16: The Sma' Still Returns

1. Report from the Select Committee of the House of Lords, appointed to consider the consequences of extending the functions of the constabulary in Ireland to the suppression or prevention of illicit distillation, *House of Commons Papers*, Vol 10 (53), 1854, evidence of John Wood, Head of the Board of Inland Revenue, p.209.
2. Reports of Cases Before the High Court and Circuit Courts of Justiciary in Scotland: During the Years 1842-1845, Vol 2, 1846, pp. 495-8.
3. Third report of the Inspectors Appointed Under the Provisions of the Act 5&6 … to Visit the Different Prisons of Great Britain. IV. Scotland, Northumberland, and Durham, *Command Papers*, Vol 31 (120), 1837-1838, pp.68-9.
4. *Glasgow Herald*, 29 December 1851.
5. Ibid.
6. Ibid.
7. Ibid.
8. Possibly Balliekine (NR 8703960), spelt Ballican on Ramsay's map from 1841.
9. *Glasgow Herald*, 29 December 1851.
10. Ibid.
11. Ibid.
12. *York Herald*, 1 December 1855.
13. *Glasgow Gazette*, 17 January 1852.
14. Ibid.

15. Ibid.
16. Ibid.
17. Ibid
18. *York Herald*, Saturday 1 December 1855.
19. Ibid.
20. Reports of Cases Before the High Court and Circuit Courts of Justiciary in Scotland, During the Years 1855, 1856 and 1857, Volume 2, 1858, p.426.
21. *Glasgow Herald*, 8 December 1858.
22. Ibid.
23. *Glasgow Free Press,* 28 May 1859.
24. Ibid.
25. *Glasgow Herald,* 28 April 1860.

Chapter 17: 'Arran Water' Today

1. MacKenzie, *The Book of Arran*, p.136.
2. A Boyd Scott, *The East of Arran*, Paisley, 1919, p.232.
3. Ibid, pp. 223-36.
4. MacKenzie, *The Book of Arran*, p.136.
5. Liz Dale, interview with G Adamson (Isle of Arran, 20 May 2015).
6. MacKenzie, *The Book of Arran*, p.213.
7. Kate Hartley, interview with G Adamson (Isle of Arran, 6 June 2015).
8. Ibid.
9. John Hartley, interview with G Adamson (Isle of Arran, 6 June 2015).
10. Allan Little, interview with G Adamson (Isle of Arran, 22 August 2017).
11. Account of Charles MacLean, quoted in, Smith, *The Secret Still*, p.107.
12. Mark Bunyan, interview with G Adamson (Isle of Arran, 21 August 2017).
13. Ibid.
14. Wilson, *The Arran Malt*, p.161.
15. *Arran Banner*, 18 February 2017.

BIBLIOGRAPHY & SOURCES

Arran Estate Office (AEO)

Account of Expenses Laid out by Robert McGregor, 30th September 1808.

Account of Money Lead out by Peter McBride for the Whitehouse Distillery, December 1794-December 1795.

Account of sundrie articles and utensils and other adornments made by Alexander McLean, for the use of Glenshant Distillery from 1 Dec 1790 to 1 Jan 1793.

Account of the expense on the seizure of two small casks of whiskie by James McBride, in the Island of Arran, 8th July 1805.

Accounts of Charge and Discharge for the Arran Estate, 1825.

Copy Memorial and Representation of James Lamont, to the Commissioners of Excise, 1808.

James and Peter McBride to Captain James Hamilton (Copy), 27 April 1793.

John Burrel's Arran Journal, Volume I, 1766-1773.

List of Arran Tenants Summoned to Appear at the Excise Court on the 9th, 10th and 12th July 1802.

Macleod Bannatyne, Edinburgh to William Stevenson, Arran Castle, 15 June 1796.

Petition of Daniel Currie, Sliddery, 12th October 1807.

Petition of John McCurdy, East Bennan, 15th December 1808.

Petition of John Murphie, West Bennan, 1806.

Petition of John Robertson, Torbeg, 18 September 1807.

Petition of Neil Cook and others, 1806.

Petition of Robert McGrigor, Excise Officer in Rothesay, 25 February 1800.

Petition of William Stuart, Benecarigan, 1807.

Rent Ledger: Arran Estate, 1823-1827.

Rent Ledger: Arran Estate, 1826-1833.

Robert Brown, Hamilton Palace to James McBride, Arran, 10 April 1813.

Robert MacGrigor to James McBride, 18 September 1793.

The Tacksmen of Benecarrigan to James Lamont, Factor in Arran, 27 March 1809.

Warrant against John Hendry in Mosend, Hugh MacKenzie Miller at Shedog, Hugh Ker Assistant Miller at Lochranza, and Neil MacCook in Slidery, April 1803.

Glasgow City Archives, Mitchell Library (GCA)

CE73/1/4: *Rothesay Outport Letter Book: Collector to the Board, 21 March 1822; Rothesay Outport Letter Book: Collector to the Board, 2 March 1816.*

CE73/1/5: *Rothesay Outport Letter Book: Collector to the Board, 21st March 1822.*

CE73/2/3: *Rothesay Outport Board's Orders: Board to the Collector,*
11 January 1799.
CE82/1/19: *Campbeltown Outport Letter Book: Collector to the Board,*
18 September 1807; Collector to the Board, 17 November 1807.
CE 82/1/20: *Campbeltown Outport Letter Book: Collector to the Board,*
9 May 1808.
CE82/1/27: *Campbeltown Outport Letter Book: Collector to the Board,*
8 August 1814.
CE82/1/30: *Campbeltown Outport Letter Book: Collector to the Board, 1 July 1817;*
Mr Anley to the Controller of Customs in Campbeltown (Copy), 1 July 1817;
Petition of Daniel Kennedy, Alex McKelvie, Allan Bailie and Alex McMillan,
Fishermen and Cotters Residing at Whiting Bay in the Island of Arran, now
Prisoners in the Tollbooth of Campbeltown (Copy), 1 July 1817.
CE82/1/31: *Campbeltown Outport Letter Book: J Aubrey, Master of H.M.S*
Driver to the Collector (Copy), 16 December 1817.
CE82/1/32: *Campbeltown Outport Letter Book: Collector to the Board,*
2 August 1819.
CE82/1/33: *Campbeltown Outport Letter Book: Collector to the Board,*
15 September 1819.
CE82/1/35: *Campbeltown Outport Letter Book: Petition of Duncan Sillars present*
prisoner in the Jail of Rothesay (Copy), 11 May 1821.
CE82/2/29: *Campbeltown Outport Board's Orders: Board to the Collector,*
13 September 1816; Capt. James Fullarton to the Collector (Copy), 13
September 1816; Board to the Collector, 18 September 1816

National Records of Scotland, Edinburgh (NRS)
CH2/214/2: *Kilmory (Isle of Arran) Kirk Session, Minutes and Poor's Fund Lists,*
1786-1854.
CS46/1836/1/87: *Decreet, Allan Fullarton Esq v Charles Macalester Shannon*
and Miss Wortley Stewart Macalester, Jan 1836.
E581/5/26: *Distillery Discharge Vouchers: Argyle South collection: Rothesay:*
rounds 5-8, 1827-1828.
E581/6/26: *Distillery Discharge Vouchers: Argyle South collection: Rothesay:*
rounds 1-4, 1828-1829.
E581/6/27: *Distillery Discharge Vouchers: Argyle South collection: Rothesay:*
rounds 5-8, 1828-1829.
E581/9/53: *Distillery Discharge Vouchers: Argyle South collection: Rothesay:*
rounds 1-5, 1831-1832.
JC12/27: *Minute Book, 26 April 1810 – October 1812.*
JC13/35: *Minute Book, 25 April 1807 – 28 September 1807.*

JC26/1809/37: *Trial papers of Alexander Stewart and Robert Stewart, sons of Donald Stewart, farmer at Largiemenoch, parish of Kilbride, Island of Arran, for the crime of assaulting, beating, and violently maltreating an officer of the Public Revenue, September 1807.*

JC26/1811/34: *Trial papers relating to Alexander Kerr senior, farmer or residenter in Kilbride in the Parish of Kilmory on the island of Arran, Alexander Kerr junior, weaver in Kilbride aforesaid, James Nickol or Nicol, weaver, in Kilbride, John Murphy residing in Kilbride and Archibald Cook, farmer, in Shanochy in the Parish of Kilmory for the crime of obstructing, assaulting, deforcing, striking and wounding officers of the Revenue, September 1811.*

RH4/42: *Robert Armour, Plumber and Coppersmith in Campbeltown: Account Books, 1811-1817.*

National Register of Archives for Scotland: Papers of the Douglas-Hamilton family, Dukes of Hamilton and Brandon. (NRAS2177)

Bundle 1576: *Robert Brown, Hamilton, to the Marquis of Douglas (Draft), 4 June 1812; William Wallace Currie Esquire to Alexander Young (Copy), 22 May 1812.*

Bundle 1672: *Dr John Stoddart to Robert Brown, 1 November 1816.*

Bundle 1675: *James Davidson to Robert Brown, 10 December 1816; Robert Brown to Matthew Brown, Corseflat, Paisley (Copy), 11 December 1816.*

Bundle 1676: *Alexander Young to Robert Brown, 15th December 1816.*

Bundle 1677: *Alexander Young to Robert Brown, 25 December 1816.*

Bundle 1678: *Alexander Young to Robert Brown, 4 January 1817; James Davidson to Robert Brown, 8 January 1817; Dr John Stoddart to Robert Brown, 13 January 1817; James Davidson to Robert Brown, 14 January 1817.*

Bundle 1679: *Dr John Stoddart to Robert Brown, 17 January 1817; Dr John Stoddart to Robert Brown, 19 January 1817.*

Bundle 1680: *Alexander Young to Robert Brown, 15 February 1817; James Davidson to Robert Brown, 16 February 1817.*

Bundle 1681: *Alexander Young to Robert Brown, 22 February 1817; Robert Brown to Alexander Young, 17 February 1817.*

Bundle 1682: *Dr John Stoddart to Robert Brown, 19 March 1817; James Davidson to Robert Brown, 2 March 1817.*

Bundle 1683: *Alexander Young to Robert Brown, 25 March 1817; James Davidson to Robert Brown, 26 March 1817; Alexander Young to Robert Brown, 31 March 1817.*

Bundle 6043: *Tenants of the Island of Arran to James Stewart, Chamberlain of Arran, 20 February 1759.*

Bundle 6163: *Specifications of the Corn Miln and Kiln intended to be built at Lagg, June 1819; Robert Brown to John Paterson on Captain Shannon's arrears, 11 November 1822; Copy Memoranda of Business adjusted with his Grace the Duke of Hamilton of Brandon, Arran Estate, 1823; Report of the Offers given for the following farms on the Estate of Arran, the property of His Grace the Duke of Hamilton and Brandon, September 1833.*

The National Archives, London (TNA)
T1/2301 (15612): *Report on Distilling in Scotland, 1824.*

Published Primary Sources
Accounts Relating to Distillery from Malt and Raw corn; Duties from Spirits Made in England, Ireland, and Scotland; Beer Made by Licensed Brewers and Victuallers; Spirits Warehoused by Each Distiller in Scotland and Ireland; the Malt Laws, *House of Commons Papers*, Vol 18 (217), 1828.
Arran Banner, 18 February 2017.
Buteshire Ordnance Survey Name Books, Vol 2, 1855-1864.
Caledonian Mercury, 22 March 1817.
Caledonian Mercury, 11 September 1817.
Chester Chronicle, 9 August 1805.
Criminal Letters His Majesty's Advocate Against Daniel Cook, Inveraray Circuit Court, 17 August 1807.
Declaration of Daniel Cook, Inveraray Circuit Court, 21 May 1807.
Edinburgh Advertiser, October 1796.
Edinburgh Gazette, 19 March 1830.
Eleventh Report of the Commissioners of Inquiry into the Collection and Management of the Revenue Arising in Ireland, Scotland, *House of Commons Papers*, Vol 13 (389), 1825.
Evening Chronicle, 1836.
Farmer's Magazine: A Periodical Work Exclusively Devoted to Agriculture and Rural Affairs, Vol 18, 1817 and Vol 19, 1818.
Fifth Report of the Commissioners of Inquiry into the Collection and Management of the Revenue Arising in Ireland; &c. Distilleries, *House of Commons Papers*, Vol 7 (405), 1823.
Glasgow Courier, 3 February 1801.
Glasgow Free Press, 28 May 1859.
Glasgow Gazette, 17 January 1852.
Glasgow Herald, 7 August 1826.
Glasgow Herald, 29 December 1851.
Glasgow Herald, 8 December 1858.
Glasgow Herald, 28 April 1860.

Glasgow Herald, 18 February 1881.

Inverness Courier, 12 December 1822.

Irvine, County of Ayrshire, *New Statistical Account*, Vol 5, 1845.

Kilbride, County of Bute, *New Statistical Account*, Vol 5, 1845.

Kilmorie, County of Bute, *New Statistical Account*, Vol 5, 1845.

Kilmorie, County of Bute, *Old Statistical Account*, Vol 9, 1793.

Licensed distillers. Returns of the Number of Licensed Distillers, Informations Laid, and Names and Residences of all Persons Licensed to Distil or Rectify Spirits, who have been convicted in the several Courts of Exchequer, from the 1st January 1827, *House of Commons Papers*, Vol 59 (384), 1828.

List of Witnesses to be Adducted Against Daniel Cook, Inveraray Circuit Court, 14 October 1807.

Magazine of Botany and Gardening, British and Foreign, Vol 2, 1834.

Malt spirits. A return of the quantity of malt spirits distilled by each distiller, upon which drawback was payable, *House of Commons Papers*, Vol 34 (248), 1831–1832.

Morning Advertiser, 23 January 1843.

Nairnshire Telegraph and General Advertiser for the Northern Counties, 23 September 1857.

Newcastle Journal, 3 October 1840.

Perthshire Courier, 6 December 1822.

Report by Her Majesty's Commissioners for Inquiring into the Licensing System, and Sale and Consumption of Excisable Liquors in Scotland, *Command Papers*, Vol 2, 1860.

Report from the Select Committee of the House of Lords, appointed to consider the consequences of extending the functions of the constabulary in Ireland to the suppression or prevention of illicit distillation, *House of Commons Papers*, Vol 10 (53), 1854.

Reports of Cases Before the High Court and Circuit Courts of Justiciary in Scotland: During the Years 1842–1845, Vol 2, 1846.

Reports of Cases Before the High Court and Circuit Courts of Justiciary in Scotland, During the Years 1855, 1856, and 1857, Vol 2, 1858.

Report Respecting the Scotch Distillery Duties, *House of Commons Papers*, Vol 119, 1798.

Saunders's News-Letter, 3 November 1821.

Scots Magazine, Vol 73, 1811.

Seventh Report of the Commissioners of Inquiry into the Excise Establishment, and into the Management and Collection of the Excise Revenue Throughout the United Kingdom. British spirits: part II, *Command Papers*, Vol 30 (8), 1835.

Staffordshire Gazette and County Standard, 8 February 1840.
The Scotsman, 13 September 1817.
The Scotsman, 8 August 1838.
Third report of the Inspectors Appointed Under the Provisions of the Act 5&6 … to Visit the Different Prisons of Great Britain. IV. Scotland, Northumberland, and Durham, *Command Papers,*Vol 31 (120), 1837-1838.
Twelfth Report of the Commissioners of Inquiry into the Collection and Management of the Revenue Arising in Ireland, Scotland, *House of Commons Papers,*Vol 14 (390), 1825.
York Herald, 1 December 1855.

Published Secondary Sources
Aiton, W, *General View of the Agriculture of the County of Bute,* Glasgow, 1816.
Alison, Sir Archibald, *Principles of the Criminal Law of Scotland,* Edinburgh, 1832.
Buchanan, R, *The Land of Lorne, Including the Cruise of the 'Tern' to the Outer Hebrides,* London, 1871.
Campbell, T, *Arran: A History,* Edinburgh, 2007.
Carlyle, T & Froude, JA, (ed.), *Reminiscences by Thomas Carlyle,* New York, 1881.
Chambers, R & Chambers, W, *The Gazetteer of Scotland,* Edinburgh, 1836.
Chatterton, E Keble, *The Fine Art of Smuggling: King's Cutters vs Smugglers, 1700-1855,* Tucson, 2008.
Devine, TM, The Rise and Fall of Illicit Whisky-Making in Northern Scotland c.1780-1840, *The Scottish Historical Review,*Vol 54 (158), 1975, pp.155-177.
Dickson, T (ed.), *Accounts of the Lord High Treasurer of Scotland,* Edinburgh, 1877.
Fraser, IA, *The Place-Names of Arran,* Glasgow, 1999.
Gemmell, A, *Discovering Arran,* Edinburgh, 1990.
Glen, Dr IA, Robert Armour: A Maker of Illicit Stills, *Scottish Studies,* Vol 14, 1970, pp.67-83.
Hamilton, JA, *Reminiscences of James A. Hamilton; or, Men and Events, at Home and Abroad, During Three Quarters of a Century,* New York, 1869.
Hunter, J, *Set Adrift Upon the World: The Sutherland Clearances,* Edinburgh, 2015.
Inglis, JC, *Brodick Old and New,* Ardrossan, 1932.
Johnson, S, *A Journey to the Western Islands of Scotland,* London, 1775.
Kennedy Cameron, J (ed.), *Gaelic and English Sermons of the Late Rev. John MacAlister, with Memoir,* Inverness, 1897.
Little, JI, Agricultural Improvement and Highland Clearance: The Isle of Arran, 1766-1829, *Scottish Economic and Social History,* Vol 19 (2), 1999, pp.132-154.

MacBride, M, *Arran of the Bens, the Glens and the Brave*, Edinburgh, 1911.

MacCulloch, J, *The Highlands and Western Isles of Scotland*, London, 1824.

MacDonald, I, *Smuggling in the Highlands: An Account of Highland Whisky with Smuggling Stories and Detections*, Inverness, 1914.

MacKenzie, WH, *The Book of Arran*, Glasgow, 1914.

Martin, A, *Kintyre Country Life*, Edinburgh, 1987.

Martin, M, *A Description of the Western Islands of Scotland*, London, c.1695.

McArthur, J, *The Antiquities of Arran: With a Historical Sketch of the Island*, Glasgow, 1861.

McLellan, R, *The Isle of Arran*, New York, 1970.

McLellan, R, The Smugglers, *Robert McLellan: Playing Scotland's Story*, Donati, Colin (ed.), Edinburgh, 2013.

Moss, M & Hume, J, *The Making of Scotch Whisky: A History of the Scotch Whisky Distilling Industry*, Edinburgh, 1981.

Paterson, J, Account of the Island of Arran, *Transactions of the Highland and Agricultural Society of Scotland*, Vol 11, 1837, pp.125-55.

Paterson, J, *Autobiographical Reminiscences: Including Recollections of the Radical Years, 1819-1820, in Kilmarnock*, Glasgow, 1871.

Paterson, J, *Reminiscences of 'Auld Ayr'*, Edinburgh, 1864.

Ramsay, AC, *The Geology of the Island of Arran from Original Survey*, Glasgow, 1841.

Rees, T & Shaw, R, *Park Terrace Corn Mill, Lamlash, Isle of Arran: Standing Building Recording and Watching Brief, Data Structure Report*, 2005.

Scott, A Boyd, *The East of Arran,* Paisley, 1919.

Scott, Sir Walter, *Heart of Midlothian*, Oxford, 2008.

Shore, CH (2nd Baron Teignmouth), *Sketches of the Coasts and Islands of Scotland, and of the Isle of Man*, London, 1836.

Sillett, SW, *Illicit Scotch*, Aberdeen, 1965.

Smith, GD, *The Secret Still: Scotland's Clandestine Whisky Makers*, Edinburgh, 2002.

Strawhorn, J, *The History of Ayr: Royal Burgh and County Town*, Edinburgh, 1989.

Thorne, Dr RG (ed.), *The History of Parliament: The House of Commons 1790-1820*, London, 1986.

Townsend, B, *Scotch Missed: The Lost Distilleries of Scotland*, Castle Douglas, 2000.

Wilson, N, *The Arran Malt: An Island Whisky Renaissance*, Castle Douglas, 2016.

APPENDIX I

Early 19th-century illicit distillers on Arran gathered from the *Account Books of Robert Armour, 1811-1817*. The location is given first, followed by the Ordnance Survey Landranger map grid reference and the names of the distillers who operated in these locations.

BENNECARRIGAN (NR 941224)
Daniel McMurchy, John Shaw, Daniel Cook.

BLACKWATERFOOT (NR 895281)
Archibald McAlister.

CLACHAIG (NR 949215)
John McCurdie, John McAlister (jnr).

CLOINED (NR 965223)
John Cook.

CORRIECRAVIE (NR 923237)
William Currie (Alexander Currie's son), Peter McKinnon, Robert Black.

DIPPIN (NS 047225)
Allan McNeil.

DOUGARIE (NR 882373)
Hector McAlister.

EAST BENNAN (NR 996 217)
James McDonald, Alexander Nicol, Alexander Miller, Archibald Taylor, Thomas McCurdie.

FEORLINE (NR 907284)
John Benetine.

KILBRIDE (NR 972213)
James McNicol.

KILPATRICK (NR 902268)
Angus McAlister.

Appendix I

LEVENCORROCH (NS 005215)
James Taylor, Donald Shaw.

MARGAREOCH (NR 941243)
Malkom Cook, John Cook, John Cook (jnr).

PENRIOCH (NR 878447)
Neil Robertson, John Kerr.

SHANNOCHIE (NR 978212)
Archibald Cook, Thomas McBride.

SHEDOG (NR 913301)
John Crawford.

SHISKINE (NR 910296)
Angus McKinay.

SLIDDERY (NR 931228)
William Jamison, John McKinnon, James McKinnon, Kinneth Currie, John McKennan (jnr), John Cook, Daniel McKinnon (son of William), Donald McIntyre, John Banatine.

TORMORE (NR 894323)
Peter Hyman.

TORRYLINN (NR 966209)
Dougal Crawford, William Jamison.

WEST BENNAN (NR 987209)
William McKinnon, Daniel Kerr, Donald McMurchy, John Kerr, John Cook, Alexander McNicol, James McDonald.

APPENDIX II

THE SMUGGLERS (*Turus do Irbhinn le Uisge-Beatha*)
Translated by J Craig

The trip I went a-sailoring
With Alister the Drover,
The squally west wind caught our sails
Our boat went nearly over.
Then heeling to the breeze that blew,
'Twas vain for the cutters to pursue
As faster than a bird e'er flew
Through smoking drift we drove her.

'Twas rare to see her snowy wake
As snarling billows maul'd her,
The fastest frigate on the seas
Could n'er have overhaul'd her;
Unreefed, unyielding on she passed
Through darkening night and strengthening blast,
While nor-west showers came scourging fast
From Goatfell's craggy shoulder.

Our skipper Ronald then arose
And said, My jolly quorum,
To raise our hopes we'll broach a cask
And drink a hearty jorum.
When through our veins we felt the heat
King's men would n'er make us retreat,
But stick in hand, would boldly meet
And well with cudgels claur 'em.

We'd dash the hopes of all who came
Intending to oppose us,
And pack them off with bleeding crests,

And torn and bloody noses.
Long-legged Crawford then got up
And caught the tiller in his grip,
Quoth he, I'll steer our trusty ship
To land e'er morning shows us.

We hid out stuff beneath the sand,
Though little that avail'd us,
Then went our weary way to town
While sorely sleep assail'd us.
Would that a better watch we set,
Though we should ne'er have slumbered yet,
Ere we allowed such rogues to get
Our store ere morning hail'd us,

Oh, rare to see the rascals run
With kegs that n'er pais duty,
'Twas Luidein laid their burdens on,
The orders came from Clootie.
His lies he glibly would relate,
How useful they were to the State,
And though they stole, 'twas to abate
Their thirst with lawful booty.

That he was aye the sinner's friend,
Their find need never fear him,
Nor need they care what might befall
So long as he was near them;
But much I fear they need not boast,
Some later day they'll count the cost
When at his hearth their toes he'll toast.
And for their labour jeer them.

INDEX

Index

Index

Index